T0332630

LEARNING WITH NESTED GENERALIZED EXEMPLARS

**THE KLUWER INTERNATIONAL SERIES
IN ENGINEERING AND COMPUTER SCIENCE**

KNOWLEDGE REPRESENTATION, LEARNING
AND EXPERT SYSTEMS
Consulting Editor
Tom Mitchell
Carnegie Mellon University

LEARNING WITH NESTED GENERALIZED EXEMPLARS

by

Steven L. Salzberg
The Johns Hopkins University

foreword by

William A. Woods
Harvard University

KLUWER ACADEMIC PUBLISHERS
Boston/Dordrecht/London

Distributors for North America:
Kluwer Academic Publishers
101 Philip Drive
Assinippi Park
Norwell, Massachusetts 02061 USA

Distributors for all other countries:
Kluwer Academic Publishers Group
Distribution Centre
Post Office Box 322
3300 AH Dordrecht, THE NETHERLANDS

Library of Congress Cataloging-in-Publication Data

Salzberg, Steven L., 1960–
    Learning with nested generalized exemplars / by Steven L. Salzberg
; foreword by William A. Woods.
        p.   cm. — (The Kluwer International series in engineering and
computer science ; SECS 100)
    Includes bibliographical references (p.   ).
    ISBN 0-7923-9110-1
    1. Artificial intelligence.   2. Machine learning.   3. Learning,
Psychology of.   4. Induction (Logic)   5. Categorization (Psychology)
I. Title.   II. Series.
Q335.S33   1990   90–34231
006.3—dc20   CIP

Printed in the United States of America

Contents

List of Figures

List of Tables

Foreword

Machine Learning is one of the oldest and most intriguing areas of Artificial Intelligence. From the moment that computer visionaries first began to conceive the potential for general-purpose symbolic computation, the concept of a machine that could learn by itself has been an ever present goal. Today, although there have been many implemented computer programs that can be said to learn, we are still far from achieving the lofty visions of self-organizing automata that spring to mind when we think of machine learning. We have established some base camps and scaled some of the foothills of this epic intellectual adventure, but we are still far from the lofty peaks that the imagination conjures up.

Nevertheless, a solid foundation of theory and technique has begun to develop around a variety of specialized learning tasks. Such tasks include discovery of optimal or effective parameter settings for controlling processes, automatic acquisition or refinement of rules for controlling behavior in rule-driven systems, and automatic classification and diagnosis of items on the basis of their features. Contributions include algorithms for optimal parameter estimation, feedback and adaptation algorithms, strategies for credit/blame assignment, techniques for rule and category acquisition, theoretical results dealing with learnability of various classes by formal automata, and empirical investigations of the abilities of many different learning algorithms in a diversity of application areas.

My interest in this area has focused on the representational issues associated with recording what is learned and hypothesizing what might be conjectured – most importantly, the recording of the various hypotheses and partial states of knowledge through which a learning machine must progress as it learns. This is an issue that manifests itself in any learning algorithm or application, but is often taken for granted and not subjected to much scrutiny in the analysis of the learning system. I find it interesting to observe the influence of representational decisions on the learning abilities of an automaton and to speculate on the learning abilities that might be achievable with more expressive representations.

One thing that I find of particular interest in Steven Salzberg's thesis is the effect of his choice of representational paradigm on the learning abilities of his system. A salient characteristic of his method is its production of extremely compact models with very high performance. This seems to result from his use of generalized exemplars in the form of "rectangular" intervals in n-dimensional space, together with the nesting of such regions to handle exceptions. A comparison of his models with other learning methods suggests that there is something special about capturing information in the form of generalizations with exceptions.

It is interesting to compare this aspect of Salzberg's systems with the inheritance of default properties subject to overriding exceptions (as found in the knowledge representation systems of many artificial intelligence research projects and expert systems applications) and with the inheritance of methods in object-oriented programming languages. In such systems, there is a heuristically motivated conclusion, based on its utility to human programmers and knowledge engineers, that expressing knowledge in the form of high level generalizations with exceptions is an effective way to capture and apply knowledge. In the results of Salzberg's experiments with Nested Generalized Exemplars, an empirical validation of the same conclusion seems to emerge from a completely different direction.

Viewing Nested Generalized Exemplars from the perspective of rules in an expert system is informative in a number of ways. For example, one can gauge the expressive power of the representation by viewing each hyperrectangle as a conjunction of bounding interval statements about each of the dimensions in the feature space. For example, a 3-dimensional hyperrectangle [x1:x2, y1:y2, z1:z2] is equivalent to characterizing a class of cases in terms of the conjunction of clauses:

$$x > x1 \text{ and } x < x2 \text{ and } y > y1 \text{ and } y < y2 \text{ and } z > z1 \text{ and } z < z2.$$

This is remarkably similar to the kinds of conditions one finds in the rules of many expert systems. (Notice that a suggestion of how such rules might be automatically induced is implicit in this observation.) Since a given output conclusion can be associated with a number of such exemplars, this system has the ability to express output decisions on the basis of disjunctions of such conditions. Furthermore, the nesting of such rules and the interpretation of the included rectangles as exceptions provides the equivalent of a negation operator. Thus, this system has the full expressive power of arbitrary Boolean combinations of feature inequalities – i.e., anything that can be said with the operators "and," "or," "not," "<," and ">."

On the other hand, there is something unique in the way that these rules are applied when new cases are encountered that do not fall within the scope of any rule (i.e., any rectangle). Specifically, the "nearest" rectangle is taken as a candidate, and if it proves successful then the corresponding rule is generalized to include the new case. Failing that, the second nearest is tried, and failing that an exception is created. If the distance to the nearest rectangle is taken as a measure of confidence in the generalization, then there is even a form of "fuzzy" membership in the induced classes. This behavior is an interesting contrast to the "brittleness" of many expert systems when faced with a case outside the scope of their rules.

All this is not to say that Nested Generalized Exemplars in their current form are the final word in the endeavor. There many interesting and unresolved questions about the nature and behavior of the current model and of possible extensions. For example, it is strange that the induced classes should be bounded by intricate nonlinear shapes in the feature space while the exceptions are crisply delimited by rectangular edges. Perhaps there should be some gradation of uncertainty in the immediate vicinity of an exception. Perhaps one should consider the relative distance of the case from the exception compared to the nearest actual exemplar in the surrounding region. (This would have consequences on the number of exemplars that have to be stored, however.)

More broadly, there are questions as to how this, or any other system that induces classes from cases, fits within the architecture of a more comprehensive learning automaton for whom the induction of classes is but one component of the overall learning activity. If the judgement of the success of an individual classification is based on its utility to the purposes of a learning agent, rather than the divine intervention of an external "expert" or the precategorization of a training set of cases, then the utility of a generalization may not be immediately apparent at the time the generalization is hypothesized. If so, then how will the learning system defer the decision whether to generalize or not until the success of the prediction becomes known? Moreover, when the evidence is finally in, how will the generalizations affected by that evidence be found and updated?

We return to the realization that we have surmounted a few obstacles in the journey, but the lofty peak is still there in the distance beckoning. The contributions of this thesis provide useful food for thought and some exciting directions for future investigation.

W. A. Woods
Harvard University
Cambridge, Massachusetts
November 1989

Acknowledgements

The process of conducting thesis research is never easy, nor is it the same for any two people who've ever done it. My trek towards a Ph.D. was a long, rather circuitous one, and I've been helped in many ways by different people. Dr. William Woods convinced me to conduct this research at Harvard, which turned out to be an excellent choice. Bill has always paid careful attention to my work, asking incisive questions, suggesting articles to read, and pointing out alternative research paths. His criticisms and encouragements have improved the work in this book enormously.

At Harvard, Professor Barbara Grosz constantly offered new perspectives on my research. She helped me to choose the research questions that I've tried to answer in this book, and she supported me in the directions I chose. She also created a thriving AI research group at Harvard, and the increased level of discussion and interaction was invaluable to me.

I also owe thanks to Professor John Daugman for serving on my dissertation committee, and for providing me with a wider range of references to the literature than I could possibly have found myself. David Aha of the University of California at Irvine sent me many important articles and provided excellent feedback about some aspects of my algorithm. Thanks to Professor David Mumford for serving on my qualifying exam committee and steering me towards important work in mathematics and statistics. Many other members of the Aiken Laboratory community at Harvard provided friendship, stimulating discussion, and insightful criticism. Many thanks go to the weekly AI group: David Albert, Cecile Balkanski, Professor Barbara Grosz, Karen Lochbaum, Joe Marks, Mark Nitzberg, Ehud Reiter, Scott Roy, and Professor Bill

Woods. Thanks also to Don Beaver, Azer Bestavros, Nicola Ferrier, Gaile Gordon, Paul Graham, Professor Abdelsalam Heddaya, Professor Mei Hsu, Dr. Michael Kearns, Professor Philip Klein, Professor Jan Komorowski, Basem Moussa, Lisa Neal, Professor Manfred Warmuth, and Professor Les Valiant. Thanks especially to my two successive office mates at Harvard, Solom Heddaya and Azer Bestavros. They acted as sounding boards for many of my ideas, in addition to providing me with countless useful programs and commands for Unix, Latex, and emacs.

During the past two years I've conducted joint work at Harvard Business School that has both enhanced my thesis work and opened up new areas of research. Thanks to Michael Watkins and Professor Jai Jaikumar for the opportunity to join them in intense, frenetic, and always exciting research. Thanks also to Professor Roger Bohn for many hours of discussions.

Reading a research book rarely tells the reader how the author conceived his ideas. My most fundamental source of ideas through the years has been my parents, Adele Salzberg and Professor Herman Salzberg. They taught me to think and ask questions, and to enjoy the pursuit of a good idea. They also encouraged and supported me uncritically for all my years of education and work. I dedicate this book to them.

My new position in the Computer Science Department at Johns Hopkins University has made completing this book as easy as such a thing can be. I feel lucky to have such energetic, inspiring colleagues in an environment where I have the freedom to pursue answers to the questions that, I expect, I will be asking for many years.

Steven Salzberg
Johns Hopkins University
Baltimore, Maryland
December 1989

LEARNING WITH NESTED GENERALIZED EXEMPLARS

1

Introduction

This book presents a theory of learning from examples called Nested Generalized Exemplar (NGE) theory, and demonstrates its importance with empirical results in several domains. Nested Generalized Exemplar theory is a variation of a learning model called *exemplar-based learning*, which was originally proposed as a model of human learning by Medin and Schaffer [1978]. In the simplest form of exemplar-based learning, every example is stored in memory verbatim, with no change of representation. The set of examples that accumulate over time form category definitions; for example, the set of all chairs that a person has seen forms that person's definition of "chair." An example is normally defined as a vector of features, with values for each feature, plus a label which represents the category of the example.

NGE theory makes several significant modifications to the exemplar-based learning model. It retains the notion that examples should be stored verbatim in memory, but once it stores them, it allows examples to be *generalized*. In NGE theory, generalizations take the form of hyperrectangles in a Euclidean n-space, where the space is defined by the variables measured for each example. The hyperrectangles may be nested one inside another to arbitrary depth, and inner rectangles serve as *exceptions* to surrounding rectangles. With respect to other machine learning theories, these nested, generalized exemplars are a novel way

1

to represent concepts.

The test of this theory, as with all machine learning theories, is its performance on real data. Until we can develop provably correct learning algorithms, all machine learning algorithms must be subject to empirical verification. In particular, a learning theory should be compared to other theories by testing it on the same data sets. Chapter 4 presents results of the NGE algorithm using three different data sets, each of which was previously used in experiments with other learning theories. The comparisons presented in that chapter show that NGE performs at least as well as other algorithms, and in one case it performs significantly better. The application domains of the three data sets are (1) predicting the recurrence of breast cancer, (2) classifying iris flowers, and (3) predicting survival times for heart attack patients. In addition to these three domains, a discrete event simulation is used as a learning domain. The simulation allows more precise experiments with the learning model and highlights some of its strengths and weaknesses.

This book addresses the type of learning in which the learner must perform a prediction or classification task. Classifications are usually statements of the form "entity e belongs to category c," while predictions typically take the form "I predict that variable y on entity e will have value v [at time t]." The theory handles prediction tasks by recasting them as classification tasks, with any real-valued variables split into discrete value ranges. For example, a prediction problem might be to determine how long a heart patient is likely to live. The same problem, re-cast as a classification task, might ask which of three categories a patient belongs to: likely to live for more than five years, likely to live for more than one year, or likely to live for less than one year. There are many distinct domains in which such predictive tasks are important: for example, consider predicting the value of stocks, predicting the condition of hospital patients, and predicting how long a trip will take along a well-known route.

Nested Generalized Exemplar theory does not cover all types of learning. For example, it does not describe learning to perform, as in learning how to play a musical instrument. Nor does it deal with learning simple facts, which may be more of a memorization process. Rather, NGE theory is a model of a process whereby one observes a series of examples and becomes adept at understanding what those examples are examples of. This process occurs in countless human activities: doctors diagnosing illnesses, maintenance engineers learning failure modes of complicated machinery, anyone learning chess, and so on.

The program which implements NGE theory in this book is called EACH, for Exemplar-Aided Constructor of Hyperrectangles. The program produces predictions and classifications based on the examples it has seen in the past. The precise details of the NGE learning algorithm will be explained in detail in Chapter 2, but briefly: the learner compares new examples to those it has seen before and finds the most similar example in memory. To determine what is most similar, a *similarity metric*, which is inversely related to a *distance metric* (because it measures a kind of subjective distance), is used. This similarity metric is modified by the program during the learning process. The term *exemplar* is used specifically to denote an example stored in computer memory. Over time, exemplars may be modified from their original form, in ways that will be explained later. Stored with each exemplar is the value of the variable that the system is trying to predict. In the simplest case, the system (or human learner, if we are considering exemplar learning as a psychological model) predicts that the dependent variable for a new example will have the same value as that stored on the closest exemplar. Exemplars have properties such as weights, shapes, and sizes — all of which can be adjusted based on the results of the prediction. The learning itself takes place only after EACH receives feedback on its prediction. If the prediction is correct, EACH strengthens the exemplar used to make it. Strengthening can occur by increasing weight or size. If the prediction is incorrect, EACH weakens the exemplar. These processes, too, will be explained in detail later.

1.1   Background

Learning from examples has been one of the primary paradigms of machine learning research since the early days of AI [e.g., Samuel 1959]. Many researchers have observed and documented the fact that human problem solving performance improves with experience. In some domains, the principle source of expertise seems to be a memory for a large number of important examples. In chess and other domains, human experts seem to have a memory of roughly 50,000 to 70,000 specific patterns [Reddy 1988, Chase and Simon 1973]. The attempts to build truly "expert" expert systems, competent natural language processing systems, planning systems, and other types of intelligent systems have often run up against the problem that it's just too hard to put enough knowledge in the computer to get it to perform truly intelligently; i.e., at the level of humans. If only we could get the machine to collect its own information, then these problems might be solvable. Or at least so we think. This line of reasoning has lead, naturally, to attempts to build machines that learn, and it is just such reasoning that has motivated many machine learning projects. As the number of projects in machine learning exploded again in the early and mid-1980's (the first wave of machine learning work came in the late 50's and early 60's, and included Samuel's work as well as Rosenblatt's perceptron learning algorithm [Rosenblatt 1958]), machine learning came into its own as a sub-field of AI. To illustrate this point, consider that at AAAI-82, there were just *two* papers on machine learning. At AAAI-83, there were 13 papers, followed by eight papers at AAAI-84. At AAAI-86, there were 24 papers. At IJCAI conferences, the number of learning papers went from 20 in 1983 to 39 in 1987. For the most part, these papers do not include those by researchers in computational theory, who deal with questions such as what is required of a learning device and what is the inherent complexity of certain formal learning tasks [Valiant 1984]. Theoretical work has also grown tremendously in recent years, some of it quite relevant to the experimental work presented here [see, e.g., Blumer *et al.* 1987].

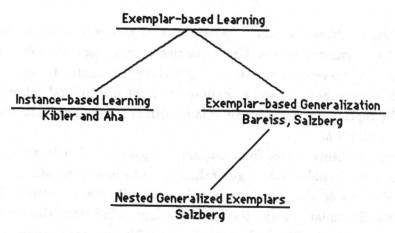

Figure 1.1: NGE as a type of exemplar-based learning.

1.2 NGE and other exemplar-based theories

Exemplar-based learning has only appeared in the AI literature in the past one or two years, and there are currently very few researchers taking this approach. However, based on the work that exists, one can construct a hierarchy of different exemplar-based learning models. The position of Nested Generalized Exemplar theory in that hierarchy is shown in Figure 1.1.

Every theory in the family shown in Figure 1.1 shares the property that it uses verbatim examples as the basis of learning; in other words, these theories store examples in memory without any change in representation. Beginning with this initial theoretical position, however, several divergent models have already appeared. A model called "instance-based learning" retains examples in memory as points, and never changes them. The only decisions to be made are which points to store and where to put them. Kibler and Aha [1987] and Aha and Kibler [1989] have created several variants of this model, and they are experimenting with how far they can go without storing anything more than points.

NGE theory adopts the position that exemplars, once stored, should be generalized. This position is shared by the developers of the Protos system [Porter, Bareiss, and Holte 1989], which stores exemplars as schema. Protos creates an abstraction hierarchy of schema whose slots have symbolic values. Generalization occurs when slot values are replaced by more general values. NGE theory, in contrast, uses slots which have numeric values, as opposed to symbols. Generalization occurs by replacing a range of values [a,b] with another range [c,d], where $c \leq a$ and $d \geq b$.

Once a theory moves from a symbolic space to a Euclidean space, it becomes possible to nest generalizations one inside the other. The capability to do this nesting is a unique contribution of Nested Generalized Exemplar theory. Its generalizations, which take the form of hyperrectangles in E^n, can be nested to an arbitrary depth, where inner rectangles act as an exceptions to outer ones. The resulting theory has the advantages of exemplar-based generalization and adds the representational capability of storing exceptions with generalizations. These advantages are discussed later in this chapter. NGE theory is intended to encompass more than just hyperrectangles: it includes all theories that create nested generalizations of any shape from exemplars. Other shapes which might be the subject of future research are spheres, ellipses, and convex hulls. However, the nested hyperrectangles created by EACH are the only current implementation of NGE.

1.3 Previous models

The two main types of learning from examples in the history of AI research are *concept learning* and *explanation-based generalization*. Both approaches will be discussed in more depth in later chapters, but in order to frame the NGE approach properly, I will briefly describe each of these now.

1.3.1 Concept learning

Concept learning (a term that originated in the psychology literature; e.g., [Bruner, Goodnow, and Austin 1956]), tackles the problem of learning concept *definitions*. A definition is usually a formal description in terms of a set of attribute-value pairs, often called *features*. For example, "electric lamp" might be defined by the attribute-value set ((purpose illumination) (power-source electricity) (has-light-bulb T) (location indoors)). (This definition is obviously over-simplified, but it is solely intended for illustration.) Through the 1970's and early 1980's, concept learning was the only approach to inductive learning, as typified by [Kibler and Porter 1983], [Mitchell 1978], [Vere 1975], and [Winston 1975]. More recently, approaches using decision trees, connectionist architectures, and hyperrectangles (exemplar-based learning) have appeared. During the time when concept learning was the main paradigm, attempts to create learning programs restricted themselves to severely constrained environments, in which, for example, the number of variables was very small, and the number of concepts to be learned even smaller (sometimes only one or two) [e.g., Winston 1975]. This approach works best for concepts that can be completely described by a conjunction of binary variables. The target of the learning system is a description of the form (A and B and (not C) ...). By examining a series of examples, each of which is categorized as either an example of the concept or a counterexample, a learning system can refine its conjunctive definition of the concept until it exactly matches the correct description.

Disjunctive concept descriptions have been much more difficult to learn, and concept learning programs have usually ignored them (there were exceptions, for example Iba [1979]). In fact, learning certain classes of disjunctive concepts has be shown to be NP-hard, although other classes are learnable in polynomial time [Valiant 1984]. This inability to learn disjunctions is not a problem for exemplar-based learning, as I show later in this chapter.

Exemplar-based learning is a kind of concept learning in which the concept definition is created from the examples themselves, using the *same* representation language. In the instance-based learning paradigm, in fact, the examples *are* the concept (no generalizations are formed). Like other concept learning theories, exemplar-based learning requires little or no domain specific knowledge.

1.3.2   Explanation-based generalization

The explanation-based generalization (EBG) approach, on the other hand, uses as much domain knowledge as possible. This approach (also called explanation-based learning) to learning has until now been the more commonly used approach in AI today (a good review is DeJong [1986], and see also [DeJong 1981, Minton 1984, Mitchell 1983].

Although the term "explanation" has been used quite carelessly in the learning literature, I will give it a precise definition here, so as to avoid confusion. When an explanation-based learning system makes a prediction, it does so based on a vector of variable values, $x_1, x_2, ..., x_n$. The most difficult problems involve a large number of such variables: HANDICAPPER [Salzberg 1983, 1985, 1986] dealt with 70 different variables, all of them binary. An explanation consists of an inference chain (which may be a proof, but may also be merely plausible reasoning) that identifies one or more of these variables x_i as the cause of the prediction failure. This subset of variables is linked by the inference chain to the correct prediction. Once the variables have been identified, the system must revise its prediction model in some way (different theories take very different approaches to this revision process) to reflect the fact that a particular set of variables is now associated with the new prediction. The paradigm used in HANDICAPPER was to create a *hypothesis* after each prediction failure. The hypothesis was essentially a new rule, which stated that a particular conjunction of variables was the cause of the outcome which had just been observed.

The difficult part of explanation-based learning is the identification of the proper set of variables to blame for a prediction failure. The number of possible subsets of the variables x_i increases exponentially with the number of variables, so this task is intractable with any brute force technique. The essence of explanation is that the system uses some domain-specific knowledge to select, from this astronomically large set of possible explanations, a few (usually just one, but sometimes two or three) plausible explanations. The domain knowledge is used to construct a proof that variables $x_i, x_j, ...$ caused the observed outcome. The knowledge that must be provided includes detailed knowledge about how each variable affects the prediction, and especially about how the input variables interact – because independence of the input variables is usually *not* assumed. (In HANDICAPPER, an assumption of independence would have been simply false.)

In addition to the combinatoric problem, there are other significant problems such as guaranteeing the consistency of all new hypotheses, but these problems have received less attention in the literature. The problems of acquiring and using domain knowledge have presented the biggest challenges.

The contributions of HANDICAPPER were to point out (1) the kinds of domain knowledge that are useful for a learning system, (2) how much knowledge is required (in some cases, a surprisingly small amount of domain knowledge gave considerable leverage), and (3) precisely how the knowledge can be applied.

Another interesting goal of explanation-based methods is that they attempt to create as concise a description as possible of the input examples. In other words, if it is possible to create a single generalization, consisting of (for example) four conjunctive terms, which is consistent with all the inputs, then EBG seeks to find that description. Exemplar-based learning may or may not do the same thing, depending on the particular implementation, but in general, exemplar-based learning *without generalization* will store many points to describe a set of examples. The NGE learning model stores points initially, but generalizes them whenever possible. This leads to significant advantages for the NGE over other exemplar-based methods in learning disjunctive concepts and exceptions, as described below.

The area of explanation-based generalization has been the focus of much research in recent years, and some progress has been made, but the problem of how to incorporate domain-specific knowledge has not been solved. If every learning program requires an enormous amount of domain knowledge before it can demonstrate good performance, then we have a chicken and egg problem: how do we get the domain knowledge into the program if the program can't learn it? Some very recent work [e.g., Danyluk 1987] attempts to solve this problem by combining exemplar models and explanation-based learning, but the problem is still far from solved.

1.4 Comparisons of NGE and other models

To characterize the theory of nested generalized exemplars I will identify several different properties of learning theories, and show how NGE differs from or compares to prior models on each of these properties. Michalski, Carbonell, and Mitchell [1983] identified three dimensions along which machine learning systems could be classified. Quinlan [1986] used these same dimensions to categorize his own work on the ID3 system. The list below includes two of these dimensions, one of Winston's [1975], and nine additional ones to define exemplar-based learning and contrast it to other kinds of machine learning theories.

1.4.1 Knowledge representation schemes

One of the most useful and interesting dimensions in classifying machine learning theories is the way they represent the knowledge they acquire [Michalski, Carbonell, and Mitchell 1983]. Many systems acquire *rules* during their learning process [e.g., Buchanan and Mitchell 1978]. These rules are often expressed in logical form (e.g., Prolog), but also in other forms, such as schemata (e.g., Mooney and DeJong's [1985] EBG system learns schemata for natural language processing). Typically, such systems will try to generalize the left hand side of rules (the antecedent in an if-then rule) so that those rules apply to as large a number of situations as possible. Some systems try to generalize the right hand side as well. For example, Mitchell, Mahadevan, and Steinberg's LEAP system [1985] learns about VLSI design by generalizing the left and right hand sides of rules. Another way to represent what is learned is with decision trees. Quinlan's ID3 [1986], and several successors to it (some of them commercial systems, such as Expert-Ease and RuleMaster), produce decision trees as their ultimate output. Decision trees seem to lack clarity as representations of knowledge: the structure of the induced trees has been shown to be confusing to human experts, especially when the effect of one variable is masked by other variables [Breiman *et al.* 1984].

Rules and decision trees do not exhaust the possible representations of the knowledge a learning system may acquire. The NGE learning model presented in this book produces neither rules nor decision trees. Instead, it creates a memory space filled with exemplars, many of which represent generalizations, and some of which represent individual examples from the system's experience. This *structured exemplar memory* (SEM) is the principle output of the learning process. The exemplars are hyperrectangles; i.e., rectangular solids in E^n. In addition, the EACH program modifies its own distance metric, which it uses to measure distances between exemplars, based on feedback from its predictions. The distance metric itself is thus another important output of the learning process. In terms of creating a SEM as its goal, the nearest AI system to EACH is Kolodner's CYRUS [1980], which created and modified memory structures representing a history of events involving the U.S. secretary of state. CYRUS used these memory structures to understand natural language. In contrast, EACH uses them to perform prediction and categorization tasks. Another contrast is the nature of the generalization process: CYRUS generalized slot values by replacing symbols with more general symbols (e.g., replace "dog" with "animal"), while EACH generalizes by expanding hyperrectangles, which corresponds to replacing ranges of numeric values with larger ranges.

1.4.2 Underlying learning strategies

Another dimension used by Michalski, Carbonell, and Mitchell in their classification of learning theories is the underlying strategy used by the learning system. Most systems fall into one of two main categories, as Quinlan has pointed out. First, there are the *incremental* learning strategies, in which systems attempt to improve an internal model (whatever the representation) with each example they process. In *nonincremental* learning strategies, a program must see all of the input examples before beginning to build a model of the domain. Most concept learning systems follow an incremental learning strategy, since the idea is to begin with a rough definition of a concept, and modify that definition over time. The NGE model of exemplar-based learning, as embodied in EACH, falls into the incremental learning category, which means that EACH's behavior is sensitive to the order of the inputs. However, it is not *necessarily* the case that NGE learning, as a theory, have this sensitivity. Let me give a brief explanation of how such an implementation of NGE might work. The shapes of the exemplars stored in memory by EACH are sensitive to the order in which the system sees the examples. This dependence is due to the fact that with each new example, EACH re-shapes existing exemplars according to the feedback it gets. When it makes a correct prediction, for example, it may expand a single hyperrectangle to include the new point. It does not save the new example, nor does it consider re-shaping other hyperrectangles. One strategy to make NGE insensitive to input order is to save all examples – following the strategy of some instance-based learning programs – and re-compute all hyperrectangles after every new example. The re-computation would have to be order insensitive, as well. Such a process is clearly much more expensive in terms of processing time and memory, but it can result in algorithms that are not sensitive to the order of the inputs.

A non-incremental learning strategy usually assumes random access to the examples in the training set. The learning systems which follow this strategy (including ID3 and Larson's INDUCE [1977] system) search for patterns and regularities in the training set in order to formulate decision trees or rules. They may examine and re-examine the training set many times before settling on a good model. This approach offers the advantage of not being sensitive to the order of the training examples. However, it introduces the additional complexity of requiring the program to decide when it should stop its analysis: for example, if a perfect decision tree (one which classifies the entire training set correctly) divides the training set into trivial categories (each containing only one example), then the system has probably divided the examples too finely and should have stopped earlier.

1.4.3 External information

Another dimension along which to array learning programs is defined by how much information beyond the examples themselves is supplied to the program [Winston 1975]. At one end of this spectrum we find pure induction, where only the examples are given to a program, and at the other end we find learning by being told, where the program is given a complete description of the target concept (or generalization). Truly "pure" induction would begin with raw sensor data, and would learn to extract higher level features from that, whereas all learning programs to date pre-define the features which they will use for learning. Winston's program (on learning the definition of an arch) fell somewhere in the middle of this spectrum, since it knew that each *negative* example differed from the target concept by exactly one term. (One could argue that this places his program quite close to the "learning by being told" model.) VanLehn's SIERRA program [1987] falls closer to the induction end of the program. It learns from "lesson sequences" – sequences of examples grouped into lessons. The program learns procedures, rather than concepts, but it fits into the general inductive learning paradigm nonetheless (the procedures are represented as ATNs). The additional knowledge the program has is that (1) each lesson corresponds to exactly one subprocedure that must be learned, and (2) the order of examples within the lesson is significant.

Exemplar-based learning, including NGE, falls very near the pure induction end of the external information spectrum, since an exemplar-based system gets examples in their natural order, and is not told anything beyond what the features are and what the correct classification should be for each example (for classification tasks). The NGE model can, of course, be modified to use additional information, such as a particular ordering of the examples, but it was designed to be as general as possible, which means it does not assume anything about the order or structure of the inputs.

1.4.4 Domain independent learning

Explanation-based generalization (EBG) [DeJong 1981, Mitchell 1983, DeJong and Mooney 1986] requires considerable amounts of domain-specific knowledge to construct explanations. Although there are common principles underlying explanation-based generalization, implementations are of necessity domain dependent. This results from the fact that explanation based systems must construct "explanations" each time they experience a prediction failure, and these explanations always draw upon domain knowledge. As a result, every explanation-based learning system is different, since every domain has its own special knowledge. Although one of the main insights of explanation-based learning work is that domain knowledge is tremendously powerful as a tool for learning, it leaves us begging the question of how the domain knowledge got into the system in the first place. My own work on explanation-based generalization [1983, 1985] led me to inquire more into paradigms for machine learning that did not require domain specific knowledge.

There has been some progress towards extracting features of explanation-based learning systems that can apply to all learning systems: for example, the second version of the HANDICAPPER program [Salzberg 1985] used a set of domain-independent heuristics to help it in constructing explanations, and others have used some of the same heuristics [Holland et al. 1986]. However, the requirement for considerable amounts of domain knowledge does constrain implementations of explanation-based learning to be domain dependent.

Exemplar-based learning does not construct explanations at all. Instead, it incorporates new examples into its experience by storing them verbatim in memory. Because it does not convert examples into another representational form, it does not need a domain theory to explain what conversions are legal, or even what the representations mean. Interpretation is left up to the users of the system, presumably domain experts. A consequence of this domain independence is that systems like EACH can be quickly adapted to new domains, with a minimum of programming. Models besides EACH which are domain independent include Quinlan's ID3 [1986], other exemplar-based learning models [Aha and Kibler 1989, Bareiss, Porter, and Wier 1987], and many connectionist models [Rumelhart and McClelland 1986].

1.4.5 Generalizations with exceptions

Perhaps the most important distinguishing feature of NGE learning is its ability to capture generalizations with exceptions. Exemplar-based learning models do not, in general, create generalizations at all. However, virtually all other learning programs do. Yet among those programs, very few represent generalizations with exceptions, as NGE does.

The generalizations created by any learning program are associated with a prediction – often in the form of a decision on category membership. The task of the learning program becomes one of placing new examples into the correct category. However, naturally occurring categories are not always easily characterized, and this has presented a major problem to generalization algorithms. Exceptions to a category have to be handled, and they often cannot be ignored. The NGE model stores exceptions and provides for the formation of a new sub-category within any existing category. EACH explicitly handles exceptions by creating "holes" in the hyperrectangles which represent generalizations in SEM. These "holes," or exceptions, are also hyperrectangles, and they can have additional exceptions inside them, nested as deep as the data require.

1.4.6 One-shot learning

Humans have a remarkable ability to learn from a single example, and this ability is one that the NGE model tries to emulate. One-shot learning refers to an ability to learn a new concept (or category) from one example. An example of this ability in humans is the well-documented ability to remember individual exceptions to widely held generalizations [Kahneman, Slovic, and Tversky 1982]. Such memories are retained despite the fact that similar exceptions may not occur for many years.

Yet this kind of ability is not demonstrated by most machine learning programs, which usually rely on notions of statistics that make one-shot learning very difficult. In a typical learning system, a statistical outlier that might be very salient to a human learner must be confirmed by additional examples before it can be utilized. In EACH, once a new point has been stored in memory (an event which is based on a single example), it is immediately available for use in prediction.

Under certain constraints, decision tree models might be able to achieve one-shot learning, by dedicating a branch of the tree to a single example. Decision tree models are typified by Quinlan's [1986] ID3 program, but there is another, more statistically oriented set of such models which go by the name Classification and Regression Trees, or CART [Breiman et al. 1984, Carter and Catlett 1987]. However, the pruning strategies necessary to improve the generality of decision trees also make it very unlikely that a single-example branch will be created. Typically, a single example which does not fit into an existing category is treated as noise. As pointed out by Quinlan, the ID3 algorithm "should refrain from increasing the complexity of the decision tree to accomodate a single noise-generated special case" [1986]. Connectionist models also have great difficulty learning from single examples. Explanation-based learning models make the best progress on this problem: some of them, by carefully attempting to explain each prediction failure, manage to extract significant amounts of information from a single example [see also Salzberg 1983].

1.4.7   Many variables, many concepts

Over the course of time, machine learning theories have gradually increased the number of concepts that they can learn and the number of variables they could process. Many early programs [e.g., Winston 1975, Mitchell 1978] could learn exactly one concept, and some programs still remain limited in this respect. Some of the theories that handle multiple concepts need to be told exactly how many concepts they are learning: for example, most clustering techniques need to know the number of clusters [Everitt 1980]. The EACH learning system will create as many concepts as it needs, while using some heuristics to keep that number to a minimum.

The number of variables handled by learning programs has also grown, but not very greatly. The problem is that with a large number of variables, very little can be learned using concept learning techniques, and explanation-based techniques tend to get overwhelmed by the amount of background knowledge required. Statistical techniques have showed some promise, but they need very large numbers of examples, preferably well distributed through the feature space, in order to produce good predictive models. Exemplar-based learning performs best with a small number of variables, as do all learning techniques, but it degrades only very gradually as it scales up to larger numbers of variables. Results in support of this claim will be presented in Chapter 4.

1.4.8 Binary, discrete, and continuous variables

One shortcoming of some learning programs is that they handle only binary variables, or only continuous variables, but not both. The EACH learning program handles variables which take on any number of values, from two (binary) through infinity (continuous). It treats binary values as having distance zero, if they are equal, and one (the maximum distance) if they are not. Discrete values are handled the same way, unless they are ordered (for example, the integers from 1 to 100 are an ordered discrete set). Ordered discrete values are treated the same as continuous values. See Chapter 2 for details of measuring distance.

It is also important to make the distinction between continuous input variables and continuous output. If a program is making category decisions, then its output is a discrete value, usually one of small set of possible values. EACH can make predictions about real-valued variables as well as discrete categories. It takes such variables and breaks them up into a set of discrete intervals, where the size of the intervals is determined by a programmer-set sensitivity factor. For example, if EACH is predicting a variable which ranges from 1.0 to 5.0, it might break it up into ranges [1.0, 1.05], [1.05, 1.10], etc. Exactly where the breaks occur is determined by the data. For example, if the first example results in an output value of 2.72, the program will create an interval [2.695, 2.745] around this value. No other machine learning program automatically segments intervals in this fashion.

1.4.9   Disjunctive concepts

Many concept learning programs have ignored disjunctive concepts because they are so difficult to learn, and explanation-based learning models have followed in the same path. As Bundy, Silver, and Plummer [1985] showed, certain sequences of examples, when presented to concept learning programs, cause an inconsistency to emerge and result in the failure of the algorithm. They and others [Thornton 1987] call this problem the "disjunctive-concept problem," since such sequences of examples may indicate the existence of a disjunctive concept.

EACH handles disjunctions very easily. It can store many *distinct* memory objects (exemplars) which carry the same prediction (i.e., they describe the same category). A new example which matches any one of these distinct exemplars will fall into the category they represent. A set of such exemplars represents a disjunctive concept definition.

The problem of learning disjunctive concepts brings up some interesting issues in complexity theory, as has been shown by Valiant [1984, 1985]. While this paper is not the place to discuss these results, a brief synopsis might be illuminating. For details, see [Valiant 1984]. Valiant has investigated the classes of propositional concepts that can be learned from examples in polynomial time. (An assumption behind this work is that concepts which cannot be learned in polynomial time are probably intractable for humans.) Some of his results on the class of concepts represented in disjunctive normal form (DNF) (generally a very useful class of concepts) show that significant subclasses of DNF expressions are learnable in polynomial time. For example, k-DNF formulae, where the number of disjuncts k is fixed, are polynomially learnable if the learning algorithm is *not* restricted to creating k-DNF formulae as its hypotheses. In addition, there are indications that significantly larger classes are NP-hard; e.g., the DNF learning problem in which the learning device is restricted to creating a formulae in k-DNF, and where the target concept is known to be in k-DNF. (These results by Valiant apply to concepts expressed in terms of binary variables.)

1.4.10 Inconsistent data

EACH does not assume that the examples it processes are consistent, and it does not falter when faced with inconsistencies. In other words, it is possible that two examples will have the same values for every variable which the system recognizes (remember that an example is simply a vector of variable values), and yet they will fall into different categories. In this situation, EACH will simply note that the exemplar used in predicting the inconsistent example has a lower probability of making a correct prediction. Every exemplar in memory, in fact, has stored in it a record of its probability of success, based on the actual use of the exemplar. EACH uses this probability information in its matching process.

1.4.11 Psychological credibility

A considerable body of research in psychology supports an exemplar model as a model of human learning [see, e.g., Barr and Caplan 1987, Medin and Schaffer 1978, Medin 1983, Osherson and Smith 1981, Smith and Osherson 1984]. In fact, psychological research served as a primary inspiration for this computational model. Although not required of a theory of machine learning, psychological credibility offers some advantages if it exists. First, if humans use a similar model, then insights gained from psychological experiments may lead to advances in exemplar-based learning programs. On the other hand, successes of exemplar-based learning programs may inspire psychological experiments. This cross-fertilization benefits both fields.

It should be made clear here that the NGE learning theory, as described in this book, is not a psychological theory. Rather, it is a particular *computational* theory of machine learning, one which offers advantages as outlined above. The acid test of such a theory is its empirical performance on real data.

1.4.12 Problem domain characteristics

In addition to characterizing the dimensions along which NGE learning offers advantages over other methods, it's also worthwhile to consider the kinds of problem domains it may or may not handle. I said above that exemplar-based learning is domain independent, which is true, but there are some domains in which the target concepts are very difficult for exemplar-based learning, and other learning techniques will perform better. In particular, exemplar-based learning is best suited for domains in which the exemplars are clusters (ideally, convex solids) in feature space, and where the behavior of the exemplars in a cluster is relatively constant (i.e., they all fall into the same category). Nested Generalized Exemplar learning works equally well when exemplars in a cluster have different behavior, because it can store clusters within clusters. On the other hand, if the exemplars are strung out along an infinite curve (for example), then the best description of the domain is the equation of that curve (which can be estimated using multiple regression analysis), rather than a set of exemplar objects. Although exemplar-based learning can handle such a domain, it will not create nearly as concise a description as a curve-fitting method will. Figure 1.2 illustrates this point.

In the figure, we see that the exemplars listed in the "bad" plot for category *a* are scattered along a line which could probably be approximated by a cubic function.

1.5 Types of generalization

To conclude this introduction, I will discuss the generalization which exemplar-based learning accomplishes. Inductive learning is often positioned primarily as a process of generalization from examples, and with good reason. Essentially, any rule (or memory structure, or decision

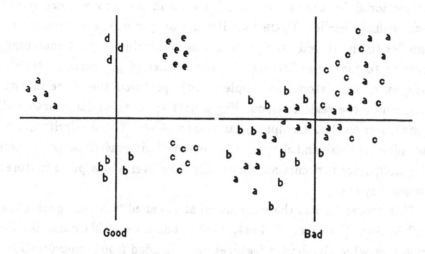

Figure 1.2: Good and bad structures for exemplar-based learning.

tree) created from a finite set of examples, which is then applied to examples not in the initial set, is a generalization. The inductive assumption is that some regularity exists in the problem domain which can be captured by the system. If the system does its job properly, this regularity can be used to classify or predict future examples in the problem domain.

The exemplar-based paradigm which I have briefly outlined thus far performs two kinds of generalization, one implicit and the other explicit. Most discussions of generalization focus on the explicit variety, but I will cover both here, since I believe the distinction is crucial when making comparisons between learning algorithms. Some algorithms perform implicit generalization only (e.g., connectionism), while others perform only explicit generalization (e.g., [Winston 1975]).

1.5.1 Implicit generalization

To illustrate the distinction more clearly, let me first explain how *implicit* generalization occurs in NGE, where it is performed by the similarity metric. Suppose we store an example in memory. If *n* is the number of features the system can recognize, then the example is a point in

n-dimensional feature space. These points in memory are *exemplars*, as was defined earlier. EACH uses its similarity metric to compare new examples to the stored exemplars and uses the closest (best matching) exemplar to make predictions. Thus the exemplars stored in feature space, even when stored as simple points, *partition* the space into regions, where the region surrounding a particular exemplar contains all points closer to that exemplar than to any other. The similarity metric determines the size and shape of this region. This generalization process is *implicit*, since it occurs automatically whenever a new point is stored in feature space.

This process is not the same as what is called "implicit generalization" in Soar [Laird *et al.* 1984, 1985]. Laird uses this name for the process by which irrelevant features are excluded from generalizations. The generalization process in Soar is called chunking, and it's essentially a method for combining rules into more efficient rules. To create a general rule from two other rules, Soar combines the antecedents ("left hand sides") of the two rules. An antecedent is typically a conjunction of tests on several variables. Implicit generalization for Laird is an effect of the way his chunking process gathers up left-hand-side conditions when it creates a chunk. The more conditions are excluded, the more general the resulting rule will be.

1.5.2   Explicit generalization

In explanation-based generalization, and in variant models such as Soar, one way of *explicitly* creating generalizations is by making constants into variables [Rosenbloom and Laird 1986]. In programs which manipulate symbolic representations, a hierarchy of symbols is used to replace symbols with more general symbols (for example, one might replace "oak" and "maple" with "wood"). In the NGE model, explicit generalization occurs by turning points into hyperrectangles, and by growing hyperrectangles to make them larger.

Explicit generalization in EACH begins when a new example falls near two or more existing exemplars. This new point is combined with

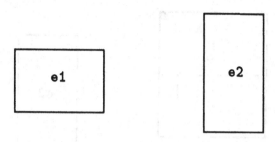

Figure 1.3: Old exemplars e_1 and e_2.

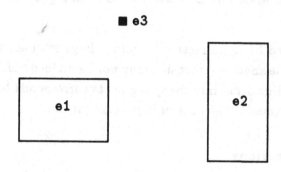

Figure 1.4: New exemplar e_3 matches e_1.

the closest existing point in memory to form a generalization which takes
the shape of a hyperrectangle; that is, an n-dimensional solid whose faces
are all rectangles. (These objects are also called *axis parallel* rectangles,
since all of the sides of the rectangles are parallel to some axis in the
space.) The closest existing exemplar may already be a hyperrectangle,
in which case it is extended just far enough to include the new point.
As far as EACH is concerned, the combination of the new point and an
existing exemplar defines a region which includes both points used to
create it. Figures 1.3-1.5 provide a graphic illustration of this process.

The generalization e_g includes a larger area than e_1, and replaces the
former e_1 region in memory.

One consequence of the exemplar-based learning model which might
be apparent here is that, over time, a particular feature (or dimension)

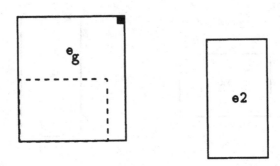

Figure 1.5: Match leads to success, so form a generalization e_g.

may be divided by hyperrectangles into a large number of very small segments, while another dimension may not be divided much at all. The division of a dimension into many segments corresponds to an expert's sensitivity to small differences in important factors.

Storing exceptions

If a new example falls inside an existing exemplar region in feature space, but the example behaves differently from others which fell in that same hyperrectangle, the learning system must recognize the new point as an exception. Once the system has realized that the new point behaves differently (or belongs in a different category), it simply stores the point. Prediction failures serve as the signal to the system that a new point does not fit into an existing category. If no more exceptions occur, the point remains a point. Suppose, however, that another exceptional point is found inside the hyperrectangle. If this second exception belongs to the same category as the first one, the two points are combined to create a small hyperrectangle inside the larger one. This new region behaves as an exception to the old generalization. Figure 1.6 illustrates, in two dimensions, what a generalization with a rectangular exception looks like in feature space.

One possible consequence of this strategy is that regions will fragment too much over time, especially if the domain in which the system

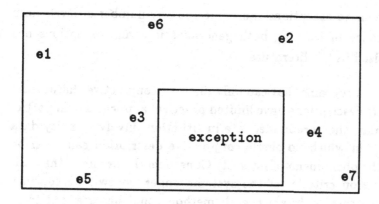

Figure 1.6: Generalization with exception.

is learning has probabilistic behavior. One possible solution to this fragmentation problem, if it occurs, is to let points decay over time, so that noisy points disappear. In all the domains I used for my experiments (discussed in Chapter 4), fragmentation was not a problem. On the other hand, we can consider probabilistic outcomes, where two examples could match *exactly*, but where they do not fall into the same category. Consider a poker hand: a hand consisting of a pair of aces, a jack, a nine, and a four might be a winning hand in one instance, and a losing hand later. In such a case, EACH will not store a new exemplar upon seeing the second example, but rather would weaken the original exemplar. Each exemplar has associated with it a weight, which is simply a number between 0 and 1 representing the proportion of the time that the exemplar made a correct prediction. (More on the adjustment and use of this weight will appear in Chapter 2.) Thus EACH's prediction, after seeing two contradictory but matching exemplars, would be that the poker hand in question wins 50% of the time, which is actually quite a reasonable way to handle the situation.

The idea of allowing exceptions to the generalizations created by an inductive learning program is an important one, but one that is difficult to accomplish when the program learns logical rules. The NGE model allows exceptions to be stored quite easily inside hyperrectangles, and exceptions to exceptions can be nested any number of levels deep. The importance of learning both generalizations and exceptions has been recognized in the literature:

> Programs that can only discover conjunctive characteristic descriptions have limited practical application. In particular, they are inadequate in situations involving noisy data or in which no single conjunctive description can describe the phenomena of interest. Consequently, as one of the evaluation criteria [of the systems under review], we consider the ease with which each method could be extended to ... discover exceptions. [Dietterich and Michalski 1983, p. 50]

In the past, many programs could perform conjunctive generalization but could not handle exceptions. The learning system described in this book has been designed specifically to handle this problem, and it will create exceptions as readily as it will create generalizations.

2

The NGE learning algorithm

This chapter describes the details of the nested generalized exemplar learning algorithm used by EACH. The text below is organized exactly in the order in which the program functions. Many variables and other features are adjustable by the user, and these are described at the points where the program would use them, rather than at the beginning. Each of the sections which follows, then, is a phase of the program's operation. For the sake of brevity, descriptions of the data structures and minor subroutines have been omitted.

Following the sections describing the individual steps in the algorithm, I give a summary and flowchart of the algorithm. This summary, which includes pseudo-code, should be sufficient to allow someone to replicate the algorithm. I also explore some implications of the distance metric as applied to hyperrectangles. In particular, I include an analysis of how the NGE algorithm partitions feature space.

2.1 Initialization

In order to make predictions, EACH must have a history of examples on which to base its predictions. Memory is initialized by "seeding" it with a small set of examples. (The minimum size of this set is one.) The discrete event simulation in Chapter 4 used between 2 and 25 examples

27

for this purpose. For the echocardiogram data, either three or four examples were used to seed memory. The seeding process simply stores each example in memory without attempting to make any predictions. An example is a vector of features, where each feature may have any number of values, ranging from two (for binary features) to infinity (for real-valued features). For example, the echocardiogram examples were patients who had recently suffered acute heart attacks, each patient being described by a vector of six variables. One of those six variables was binary, one was an integer ranging from 1 to 90, and the others were real-valued. In addition, each exemplar has a slot containing the prediction associated with that example. This prediction variable may be binary, discrete, or continuous, and the system will try to predict it accordingly. For continuous variables, the system has an error tolerance parameter, which indicates how close two values must be in order to be considered a "match." This parameter is necessary because for real-valued variables, it is usually the case that no two values ever match exactly, and yet the system needs to know if its prediction was close enough to be considered correct. For example, if the user sets the error tolerance to 1%, and an exemplar e makes the prediction 5.0, then any value in the range [4.95, 5.05] will be considered a match. If a new example has the value 5.03 for its prediction variable, and this example matches e, EACH will not store a new point in memory. The result is that continuous predictions are approximated by a discrete set of values.

The seed examples are used as the basis of memory, and memory is used to make predictions. The seeds may be scattered widely or tightly bunched, since they are chosen at random. However, in all the tests performed to date, with small and large numbers of seeds, the arrangement or choice of seeds has had little or no effect on the program's learning performance.

After initial seeding, the system begins its main processing loop.

2.2   Get the next example

The first step in the main loop is fetching the example. Naturally, the user must write some customized code to make the program convert data formats for each new data set.

The system keeps a number of statistical measures on all the examples it has seen. For example, it keeps track, for every feature which has numeric values, of the maximum and minimum values experienced for those features. These values are used to scale the features in the distance calculations, as described below.

2.3   Make a prediction

The new example is now matched to memory, using the matching process described below. Because memory has remained small in all the tests run so far, it has been acceptable to require the system to compare the new example to every object in memory. For the echocardiogram data, memory never grows beyond about 20 objects. For some larger data sets, memory has grown to a few hundred objects. The best match is then used to make a prediction in the obvious way: the system predicts that the new example will have the same value for that slot as the best matched exemplar fetched from memory. In one incarnation of EACH, the system performed a least-squares fit of the points inside each exemplar to compute predictions, rather than simply predicting that new examples would have the same value as the one previously stored. This variation required that each exemplar memory object keep a list of all points which had matched it. The results using this technique were disappointing, so it was abandoned in favor of the much simpler method described here.

2.3.1   The matching process

The matching process is one of the central features of the algorithm, and it is also a process which allows quite a bit of customization, if desired. This process uses the distance metric to measure the distance (or similarity) between a new data point (an example) and an exemplar memory object (a hyperrectangle in E^n). For the remainder of this section, I will refer to the new data point as E and the hyperrectangle as H.

The system computes a match score between E and H by measuring the Euclidean distance between the two objects. Consider the simple case where H is a point, representing an individual example. The distance is determined by the usual distance function computed over every dimension in feature space, with a few additions which are explained below:

$$D_{EH} = w_H \sqrt{\sum_{i=1}^{m}(w_i\frac{E_{f_i} - H_{f_i}}{max_i - min_i})^2}$$

where w_H is the weight of the exemplar H, w_i is the weight of the feature i, E_{f_i} is the value of the ith feature on example E, H_{f_i} is the value of the ith feature on exemplar H, min_i, max_i are the minimum and maximum values of that feature, and m is the number of features recognizable on E.

The best match is the one with the smallest distance. A few special characteristics of the computation, which are not evident in the formula above, deserve mention here. First, let's suppose we measure the distance between E and H along the dimension f. Suppose for simplicity that f is a real-valued feature. In order to normalize all distances, so that one dimension will not overwhelm the others (very likely when features may have a different units, e.g., meters, seconds, years), the maximum distance between E and H along any dimension is 1. To maintain this property, the system uses its statistics on the maximum and minimum values of every feature. Suppose that for E, the value of f is 10, and for H, the value of f is 30. The unnormalized distance is therefore 20. Suppose further that the minimum value of f for all exemplars is 3, and the maximum value is 53. Then the total range of f is only 50, and the normalized distance from E to H along this dimension is 20/50, or 0.4. (Note: another way to normalize values is to use the standard deviation as one unit, and to measure distances in terms of that. However, if values for a dimension do not follow a normal distribution, the standard deviation is not an appropriate unit.)

Because the maximum and minimum values of a feature are not given *a priori*, the distance calculation will vary over time as these values change. This variation is a direct consequence of the incremental nature of the algorithm. If the maximum and minimum values are known ahead of time, then the distance calculation will not suffer this variation.

Now consider what happens when the exemplar, H, is not a point but a hyperrectangle, as is usually the case. In this case, the system finds the distance from E to the nearest face of H. There are obvious alternatives to this, such as using the center of H (as with the centroid method in cluster analysis [Everitt 1980]), but these lead to complications if the algorithm allows the nesting of exemplars inside one another. The formula used above changes because H_{f_i}, the value of the ith feature on H, is now a range instead of a point value. If we let H_{lower} be the lower end of the range, and H_{upper} be the upper end, then our equation becomes:

$$D_{EH} = w_H \sqrt{\sum_{i=1}^{m} (w_i \frac{dif_i}{max_i - min_i})^2}$$

where

$$dif_i = \begin{cases} E_{f_i} - H_{upper} & E_{f_i} > H_{upper} \\ H_{lower} - E_{f_i} & E_{f_i} < H_{lower} \\ 0 & \text{otherwise} \end{cases}$$

The distance measured by this formula is equivalent to the length of a line dropped perpendicularly from the point E_{f_i} to the nearest surface, edge, or corner of H. This length is modified by the weighting factors, as described below.

For binary features, the distance computation is much simpler: if the features are equal, the distance is zero, else it is one. The same computation applies to any discrete, non-numeric features.

Notice that there are two weights on the distance metric. w_H is a simple measure of how frequently the exemplar, H, has been used to make a correct prediction. In fact, the use of this weight means that the

distance metric measures more than just distance. w_H is an measure
the *reliability*, or the probability of making a correct prediction, of each
exemplar. This weight measure says, in effect, "in this region of feature
space, the reliability of my prediction is n," and of course EACH wants
to maximize its success rate, so it should prefer more reliable exemplars.
The distance metric accomplishes this as follows. Suppose, in the above
example, that H had been used for 15 previous predictions, and that it
had been correct on 12 of those occasions. The system will multiply the
weight of the total match score between E and H by 15/12, or 1.25. Thus
weight is a non-decreasing function of the number of times an exemplar
has been used. If the exemplar *always* makes the correct prediction,
then the weight will remain at 1. (Note that the seed exemplars do not
get a weight of zero because they are treated as if they had predicted
themselves correctly; i.e., they are marked as having been used once and
having been correct once.) More generally, if the weight of an exemplar
is n/c, then when it is used to make an *incorrect* prediction, its weight
increases from n/c to $(n+1)/c$. If it is used to make a *correct* prediction,
its weight will increase to $\frac{n+1}{c+1}$. Note that if $n = c$, the weight will remain
at 1 after a correct use of the exemplar H.

Also, as the number of correct uses of H increases, the effect of an
incorrect use decreases: if H has been correct 100 times, and its weight
is $n/100$, then an incorrect use makes the weight $(n+1)/100$. This is an
increase of 0.01 in absolute terms. If H has only been correct 10 times,
its weight will increase from $n/10$ to $(n+1)/10$, an increase of 0.1. In the
former case the effect of an incorrect use is much smaller. This effect is
desirable because as we know more about H, we do not want a single
new example to change significantly our confidence in it.

Furthermore, noisy exemplars will gradually "disappear" as their
weight w_H increases. If a point represents noise, then its prediction will
rarely be correct for other points nearby. If such an exemplar is used
10 times, for example, but is only correct once, then its distance to new
points will be multiplied by 10. Rectangular exemplars will be affected
in the same way – large weights will make them seem very distant from
new examples. New points will be much more likely to match some

other point in memory than a noisy one.

In the experimentation with EACH, the use of this weight measure seemed to improve the performance of the system significantly. Very recently, Aha and Kibler [1989] have used a similar weight measure to create an instance-based learning system which tolerates noise.

The other weight measure, w_i, is the weight of the ith feature. These weights are adjusted over time, as described below. Since the features do not normally have equal predictive power, they need to be weighted differently (after normalization). In practice, the system performed best if these weights were adjusted for a fixed number of examples, and then locked in. When feature weight adjustment was allowed to continue indefinitely, the algorithm tended to oscillate, since adjustments in these weights can wipe out previous learning by negating the effects of previous adjustments.

2.4 Feedback

Next, EACH compares its prediction to the actual result. Here the system's behavior forks, depending on the result of this comparison.

2.4.1 Correct prediction

If EACH makes the correct prediction, it records some statistics about its performance and then makes a generalization. Two objects, E and H (using the same notation as above), are used to form the generalization. H is replaced in memory by a larger object that is a generalization of E and H. H may have been a single point, or it may have been a hyperrectangle. (After a single generalization, an exemplar becomes a hyperrectangle.) If H was a hyperrectangle, then for every feature of E which did not lie within H, H is extended just far enough so that its boundary contains E. If H and E were both points, H is replaced by a new object which has, for each feature of E and H, a range of values defined by E and H. For example, in a simple case with just the two features f_1 and f_2, if E was at (2,5) and H was a point at (3,16), then the new object would be a rectangle extending from 2 to 3 in the f_1 dimension and from 5 to 16 in the f_2 dimension.

One consequence of this generalization procedure is that all hyper-rectangles created by EACH are *axis-parallel* hyperrectangles, because they are not rotated by the algorithm. Another consequence is that growing an exemplar H1 may cause it to overlap an existing exemplar H2. The system makes no attempt to avoid this: if an example falls within an area where two hyperrectangles overlap, the system matches it to the *smaller* exemplar (this preference is merely a heuristic, based on the assumption that larger exemplars may have been over-generalized). If the system's preference leads to an incorrect prediction, the exemplar responsible is shrunk, as described below.

2.4.2   Incorrect prediction

If the system makes the wrong prediction, it has one more chance to make the right one. This "second chance" heuristic (which is intended to be nothing more than a heuristic) is used by EACH in order to avoid creating more memory objects than necessary. The idea is to try very hard to make a generalization, and thus keep down the size of memory. So, before creating a new exemplar, EACH first looks at the *second best match* in memory. Assume here that H_1 was the closest exemplar to E and H_2 was second closest. If using the second best match, H_2, will give the correct prediction, then the system tries to adjust hyperrectangle shapes in order to make the second closest exemplar into the closest exemplar. It does this by first creating a generalization (using the process outlined in the previous section) from H_2 and E. It then *specializes* the (formerly) best matching exemplar, H_1, by reducing its size. It reduces the size of H_1, which must be a hyperrectangle (if not, then the system does nothing), by moving its edges away from the new exemplar just far enough so that H_2 becomes closer along that dimension. (See the pseudocode in the following section for details of the specialization mechanism.) This process is basically a stretching and shrinking operation: H_2 is stretched, and H_1 is shrunken, in order to change the order of the match the next time around. The goal of this process is to improve the predictive accuracy of the system without increasing the number of exemplars stored in memory. Notice that shrinking an existing exemplar loses information, since shrinking pulls the boundaries of a hyperrectangle back, leaving points outside that were known to belong inside. A modified version of the EACH algorithm which avoids this problem is described with the echocardiogram results below.

A very important consequence of this "second chance" heuristic is that it allows the formation of hyperrectangles within other hyperrectangles. If a new point p1 lies within an existing rectangle, its distance to that rectangle will be zero. Its distance to another point p2 (a previously stored exception) within the rectangle will be small but positive. Thus EACH will first assume that the new point belongs to the same category as the rectangle. If p1 is in the same category as p2, then the second chance heuristic will discover this fact, and form a rectangle from these two points.

If the second best match also makes the wrong prediction, then the system simply stores the new example, E, as a point in memory. Thus E is made into an exemplar which can immediately be used to predict future examples, and can be generalized and specialized if necessary. This new exemplar may be *inside* an existing exemplar H, in which case it acts as an exception to, or "hole" in H.

EACH adjusts the weights w_i on the features f_i after discovering that it has made the wrong prediction. Weight adjustment occurs in a very simple loop: for each f_i, if E_{f_i} matches H_{f_i}, the weight w_i is increased by setting $w_i := w_i(1 + \Delta_f)$, where Δ_f is the global *feature adjustment rate*. A typical value used for Δ_f is 0.05. An increase in weight causes the two objects to seem farther apart, and the idea here is that since EACH made a mistake matching E and H, it should push them apart in space. If E_{f_i} does not match H_{f_i}, then w_i is decreased by setting $w_i := w_i(1 - \Delta_f)$. If EACH makes a correct prediction, feature weights are adjusted in exactly the opposite manner; i.e., weights are decreased for features that matched, which decreases distance, and increased for those that did not. Recall that each weight w_i applies uniformly to the entire feature dimension f_i, so adjusting w_i will move around exemplars everywhere in feature space. Thus this weight must be adjusted gradually, in order to avoid oscillation that would cancel the effects of earlier learning.

At this point, the prediction-generalization loop continues by returning to the beginning of the main loop, if the user has specified that more examples should be processed.

2.5   Summary of algorithm

This section summarizes, as concisely as possible, the algorithm described in the preceding sections. The accompanying flowchart, in Figure 2.1, presents the same flow of control and data.

As the flowchart shows, the systems reads examples from a database. Each example is a vector of feature values plus an associated prediction or category decision. Thus an example may be nothing more than a list of numbers. The output of the system is both a prediction and a modified memory space. The storage of the exemplars in memory is left to the discretion of the implementor; a simple list will suffice. EACH stores exemplars in a flat list, with the exception of nested exemplars, which are stored inside each other. In other words, to get to an exemplar e which is contained inside f, you have to find f first. This storage scheme allows more efficient search; however, none of the test applications required enough search to make this an issue. The algorithm below omits the details of the function for finding the closest match.

Given these descriptions of memory, I can now give a pseudo-code description of the algorithm. Some procedures, such as those for adjusting weights, are described in the preceding text, so I have omitted their definitions.

```
begin
    Number_of_seeds := 5;              /* Size of seed set */
    for i from 1 to number_of_seeds do
        Store_in_memory(fetch_next_example);
    /* Begin main loop */
```

```
      print(''Do you want to process another example?'');
      read(answer);
      if (answer = ''yes'') then
         begin
            e_i := (fetch_next_example);
            process_one_example(e_i);
         end;
end.


/* the procedure process_one_example does all of the
   processing for a single example */

procedure process_one_example(e_i);
begin
   /* find the two closest matches to the new example */
   M1 := find_closest_exemplar(e_i,*global_memory*);
   M2 := find_second_closest_exemplar(e_i,*global_memory*);

   /* predictions are stored with exemplars */
   P1 := get_prediction(M1);
   P2 := get_prediction(M2);

   /* the example has its classification stored with it */
   result := get_classification(e_i);

   print(''Prediction is '', P1);
   if (P1 = result) then
      begin
         adjust_weight_for_success(M1);
         generalize_exemplar(M1,e_i);
      end
   else
      begin
         adjust_weight_for_failure(M1);
         if (P2 = result) then
            begin
                adjust_weight_for_success(M2);
```

```
                    generalize_exemplar(M2,e_i);
                    check_for_overlap(M2,M1);
                end;
            else
                begin
                    adjust_weight_for_failure(M2);
                    /* store the example as a new exemplar */
                    store_in_memory(e_i);
                    adjust_feature_weights(e_1,M1);
                end;
        end;
end.          /* fetch_next_example */
```

/* The procedure generalize_exemplar extends a
   hyperrectangle H just far enough to include a new
   example e, where e is a point. This procedure can
   also handle the case where H is a point. I have
   omitted details of some sub-procedures. */

```
procedure generalize_exemplar(H,e);
begin
    for i from 1 to *number_of_features* do
        begin
    /* feature(i,e) retrieves the value of feature i on
       a point e, and it retrieves an interval if e is a
       rectangle.  lower_end and upper_end return a pointer
       to the lower and upper values of an interval.  */
        if feature(i,e) < lower_end(feature(i,H))
        then lower_end(feature(i,H)) := feature(i,e)
        else if feature(i,e) > upper_end(feature(i,H))
                then upper_end(feature(i,H) := feature(i,e));
        end;
    end.      /* generalize_exemplar */
```

/* The procedure check_for_overlap takes two
   hyperrectangles, H1 and H2, where it is known that H1

```
     just made a correct prediction for a point on which
     H2 made a mistake.  If H1 and H2 overlap, this
     procedure shrinks H2 until it is just adjacent to H1. */

procedure check_for_overlap(H1,H2);
begin
   for i from 1 to *number_of_features* do
     begin
     /* interval_overlaps is a predicate which checks if
      its first argument, which is a interval, includes
      part (not all) of the second argument, which is
      also an interval.  */
      fH1 := feature(i,H1);
      fH2 := feature(i,H2);
      if interval_overlaps(fH1,fH2)
      then
         if upper_end(fH1) > lower_end(fH2)
         then lower_end(fH2) := upper_end(fH1)
      else  /* it must overlap the other way, so ... */
         upper_end(fH2) := lower_end(fH1);
     end;
end.        /* check_for_overlap */
```

2.6 Partitioning feature space

Using a Euclidean distance formula to determine similarity effectively
partitions the feature space among the exemplars. I mentioned this
partitioning briefly in Chapter 1, in the section on "implicit" generalization. In this section, I give a closer analysis of how the exemplars
divide feature space. As I will show, the partitioning is very complex,
even with only two dimensions and two exemplars. (All of the partitioning is implicit.) With many dimensions and many exemplars, as in
the domains used to test the EACH algorithm, the partitioning is too
complex to illustrate on paper. The figures and equations shown here

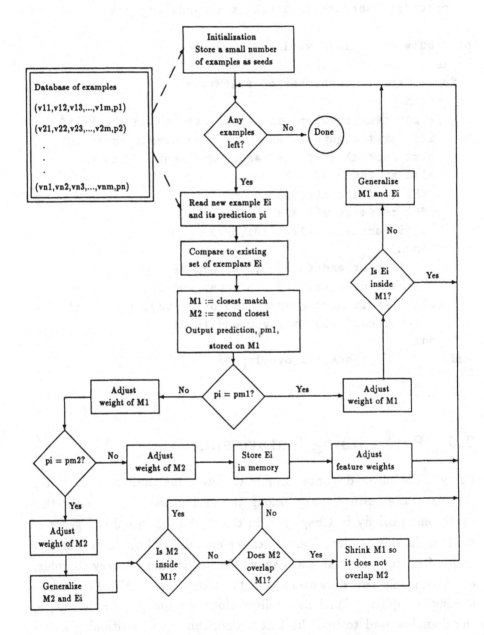

Figure 2.1: Flowchart of EACH algorithm.

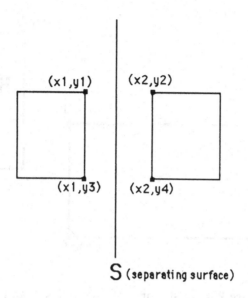

Figure 2.2: Two simple rectangles.

will thus be restricted to two dimensions and two exemplars. It should become clear that the EACH representation is equivalent to partitioning a space with many hypersurfaces, where the surfaces are not, in general, parallel to the axes – despite the fact that the rectangles themselves are always axis-parallel.

2.6.1 Simplest case

First consider what is perhaps the simplest example using rectangles, illustrated in Figure 2.2. The figure shows two rectangles, A and B, which are the only rectangles in feature space. These two rectangles divide feature space into two half-planes, separated by a surface which we shall call S for this and the subsequent examples. Recall that the distance metric takes a new example and finds the closest exemplar (either a point or a rectangle) in feature space. The metric defines S, since S is the surface of points equidistant to two exemplars in space. In this case, rectangle A has its upper border at y_1 and its lower border at

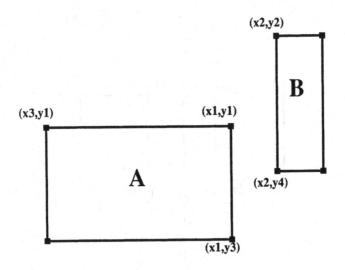

Figure 2.3: Basic form of rectangles A and B.

y_3, B has boundaries at y_2 and y_4, $y_1 = y_2$, and $y_3 = y_4$. For these two rectangles, because of the alignment of the top and bottom borders, S is simply the vertical line midway between them, as shown in the figure. Here, S is defined by $x = 1/2(x_2 - x_1)$. The width of the rectangles does not affect S. If both exemplars were points instead of rectangles, S would also be a simple line.

2.6.2   Two rectangles in two dimensions

For the second example, two rectangles shall be used again, in two dimensions, but with some very small differences from the above examples. These differences will be enough to greatly complicate the shape of S. Again, the rectangles will be called A and B, where A and B represent the categories denoted by each rectangle. These rectangles are illustrated in Figure 2.3. For the remainder of this discussion, the corners of A and B need to be labelled as shown in the figure. In particular, the upper right corner of A is the point (x_1, y_1), the upper left corner of A is (x_3, y_1), the lower right corner is (x_1, y_3), the lower left corner of B is (x_2, y_4), and the upper left corner of B is (x_2, y_2). The rectangles

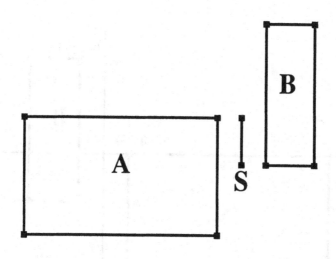

Figure 2.4: Vertical segment of S.

overlap along the y dimension; i.e., $y_3 < y_4 < y_1 < y_2$. They do not overlap on the x dimension; i.e., $x_3 < x_1 < x_2$. (If the rectangles did not overlap along the y dimension, the analysis, though simpler, would be very similar to what follows here.) The surface S defined by the points equidistant to these two rectangles has several distinct pieces; in fact, it has nine different sections, alternating straight lines and parabolas, which will be described one at a time. The points where these sections meet will be termed *junctions* in the text below.

First section of S

The simplest part of the surface is where the rectangles overlap, at $y_4 < y < y_1$. Here, S is simply a vertical plane, as shown in Figure 2.4. This portion of S is defined by $x = 1/2(x_2 - x_1)$.

Second section of S

As we move up the y axis tracing out S, the first junction occurs at $y = y_1$. For $y_1 \leq y \leq y_2$, the distance of all points to rectangle B is just the distance along the x axis, $x_2 - x$. The distance to A, however, is the

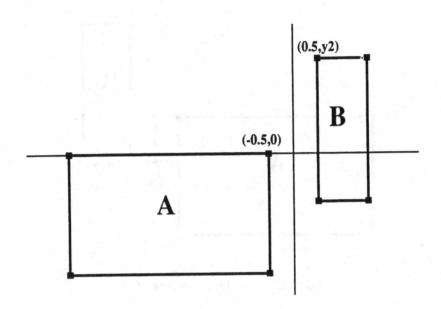

Figure 2.5: Shifted axes.

distance to the corner(x_1, y_1), as long as $x > x_1$, so that distance will be $\sqrt{(x - x_1)^2 + (y - y_1)^2}$. What happens here is that S pivots around the corner (x_1, y_1), giving us a parabola (recall that one definition of a parabola is the set of points equidistant to a point and a line). S is thus defined as

$$x_2 - x = \sqrt{(x - x_1)^2 + (y - y_1)^2}$$

for $y_1 \leq y \leq y_2$, $x_1 < x$. We can manipulate this algebraically to get

$$(x_2 + x_1 - 2x)(x_2 - x_1) = (y - y_1)^2.$$

Then, without loss of generality, we can move our axes so that $x_1 = -1/2$, $x_2 = 1/2$, and $y_1 = 0$, as shown in Figure 2.5. This makes the equation of S simply

$$-2x = y^2$$

which is a left-facing parabola. This new section of S is illustrated in Figure 2.6. This parabolic section ends either when $x = x_1$ or when $y = y_2$, whichever happens first, which will depend on the relative sizes

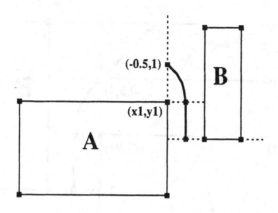

Figure 2.6: Parabolic segment of S.

of the rectangles A and B. For this example, we shall assume that the parabola ends at $x = x_1$. The value of y at this point is obtained by substituting back into our equation:

$$(x_2 + x_1 - 2x_1)(x_2 - x_1) = (y - y_1)^2$$

$$y = x_2 - x_1 + y_1$$

If we shift the axes as described above, the parabola ends at $y = 1$. The slope of the parabola here, at the point (-1/2, 1), is -1. We will see below that the next section of S has a slope of -1, which means that the junction here is smooth.

Third section of S

Continuing north along the y-axis, we come to the region where $x_2 - x_1 + y_1 < y < y_2$ and $x_3 < x < x < 1$, as illustrated by the shaded region in Figure 2.7. In this region, distance to rectangle B is just the distance along the x axis, $x_2 - x$, and the distance to A is simply the distance along the y-axis, $y - y_1$, so the equation for S is very simple:

$$y - y_1 = x_2 - x$$

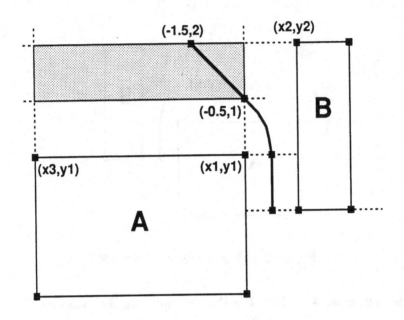

Figure 2.7: Third segment of S.

$$y = -x + x_2 - y_1$$

which is simply a line with slope -1. As stated above, this slope makes it continuous with the previous section of S. This line segment ends at one of two points, again depending on the relative sizes of A and B. These points are either at the line $y = y_2$, as is shown in Figure 2.7, or at the line $x = x_3$. The point of intersection shown in the figure is $(x_2 - y_1 - y_2, y_2)$. If, for example, we let $y_2 = 2$, then this junction point is (-1.5,2).

Fourth section of S

Moving up the y axis and left along the x axis, we now consider the points where $y > y_2$ and $x_3 < x_2 - y_1 - y_2$. In this region, S will pivot again, this time around the point (x_2, y_2). S consists of points equidistant to that point and the rectangle A, where distance to A is measured as the perpendicular distance within this region. The equation

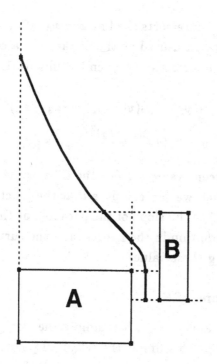

Figure 2.8: Fourth segment of S.

for S is given by:

$$(y - y_1) = \sqrt{(x - x_2)^2 + (y - y_2)^2}$$

which reduces to

$$(y_1 + y_2 - 2y)(y_1 - y_2) = (x - x_2)^2$$

As before, without loss of generality, we can see that this is a parabola by moving the axes so that $x_2 = 0, y_1 = 1/2$, and $y_2 = -1/2$, which would make the equation for S simply $y = x^2/2$, an upward-facing parabola. This section of S is drawn in Figure 2.8. If we continue to use the earlier assumptions that $x_1 = -1/2$, $x_2 = 1/2$, and $y_2 = 2$, then we can compute the slope of this parabola at the junction where it meets the previous section of S. This junction is the point $(-3/2, 2)$, and the slope is -1, which means we again have a smooth curve. This parabolic part

of S continues until it intersects the line $x = x_3$, after which distance to
both A and B will be measured as the distance to a corner point. The
y-coordinate of this intersection is given by substituting in the previous
equation:

$$(y_1 + y_2 - 2y)(y_1 - y_2) = (x_3 - x_2)^2$$

$$y = 1/2(\frac{(x_3 - x_2)^2}{y_2 - y_1} + y_1 + y_2)$$

I will call this intercept value y_5. For the sake of the example, assume
that $x_3 = -4.5$. Then we can compute that the junction point (x_3, y_5)
is simply $(-4.5, 7.25)$. The slope of the parabola at this point is -5/2. I
have used this assumption in the figures, and the curve in Figure 2.8 is
drawn to scale using these values.

Remaining sections of S

Finally, for $x < x_3$ and $y > y_5$, S is simply the straight line beginning
at the point (x_3, y_5). This line is the set of all points equidistant from
the corner (x_3, y_1) of rectangle A and (x_2, y_2) of rectangle B. This is
illustrated in Figure 2.9. Using the previous assumptions about x_3, $y1$,
x_2, and y_2, the equation for this line is

$$y = -5x/2 - 8$$

Since the slope of this line, -5/2, equals the slope of the previous parabolic section at the point (x_3, y_5), we again have a smooth curve at the
junction point.

   We have so far defined five line segments, dividing the plane for all
$y > y_4$. For $y < y_4$, we can define a similar set of line segments using
an analogous line of reasoning to that above. The very first segment we
defined, the vertical line at $x = 1/2(x_2 - x_1)$, serves as its own mirror,
so S has a total of nine segments, with eight junctions. Every junction
is smooth, so S has a continuous derivative. Note, however, that the
infinite straight line extensions at either end of S are neither colinear
nor parallel. Figure 2.10 gives the complete picture. For two rectangles,
S is a surface defined by five straight line segments and four parabolic

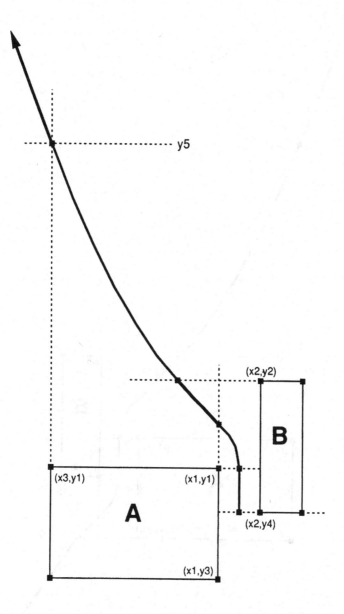

Figure 2.9: Fifth segment of S.

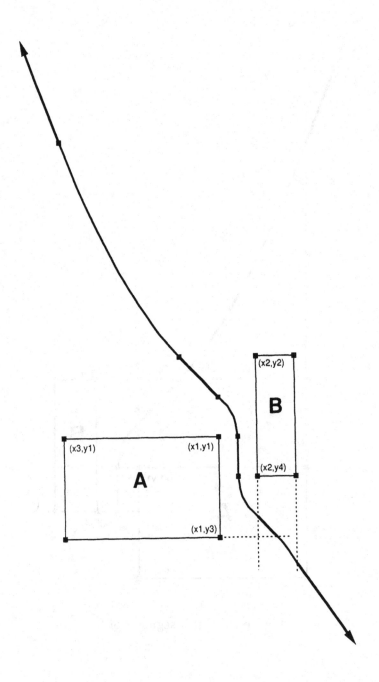

Figure 2.10: The separating surface S.

segments. This partitioning of the plane is considerably more complex than the partitioning induced by a pair of points or circles.

The purpose of this discussion has been to make it more clear how the EACH algorithm partitions feature space. The EACH algorithm does more than generate hyperrectangles, of course: each exemplar has a weight associated with it, and the feature dimensions have their own weights, all of which are modified during the learning process. The results of these weight modifications change the shape of S, but not the nature of its sections; that is, a parabolic section remains parabolic, although it may be elongated. When hyperrectangles are nested, the inner rectangle is simply a sharp-edged hole in the outer one, so the distance metric does not come into play. In a domain for which EACH creates very closely packed hyperrectangles, it is possible that all new examples will fall inside existing hyperrectangles, in which case implicit generalization does not play a role. The iris flowers domain was structured in this way. This discussion should make it easier to compare EACH to learning algorithms that form different types of clusters (e.g., ellipsoids) or that explicitly partition space with hyperplanes.

2.7 Assumptions

Several assumptions must hold in order for the NGE algorithm to function properly. None of these assumptions are very strong, and all of them are largely shared by other machine learning algorithms; nevertheless, it is worth making them explicit.

The first assumption is that the features are relevant to the prediction or category decision. If the features are completely irrelevant, then one would expect the algorithm's performance to be equivalent to random guessing. If some of the features are relevant and others are irrelevant, then the algorithm's performance will be degraded accordingly.

The next assumption is that the rules governing the problem domain are stable over time. Because past experience is the basis of all future predictions, the past must be known to be a reasonable model of the future. In other words, the rules of the game cannot suddenly change; if they do, then the algorithm must start over again to learn a new domain model. Most real domains satisfy this assumptions. An example of an exception might be treating a bacterial infection where the bacteria occasionally mutates into a different form.

One last assumption is that, because the predictions are made using a nearest neighbor approach, the feature space must be at least locally "proximal" (see Salzberg [1986] for a discussion of a proximity heuristic). Points which lie very close to each other should belong in the same category. Discontinuities do not present a problem, because the algorithm can create adjacent rectangles for distinct categories. However, if there are no continuous regions of space, then any approach which creates clusters will not work. To date, this assumption applies to all machine learning algorithms which deal with continuous variables.

2.8   Greedy variant of the algorithm

A modification of the basic algorithm was developed in order to maximize the *post hoc* success rate on the echocardiogram data, as reported in Chapter 5. This modified algorithm always creates a new exemplar after making a mistake, as opposed to checking the second closest match and adjusting the boundaries of existing exemplars. It tends, therefore, to create more exemplars than the original algorithm, so I call this version Greedy EACH (because it is greedy with memory).

The Greedy EACH algorithm was intended to be a compromise between the goal of creating a perfect *post hoc* model and that of creating useful generalizations. Its main feature was the lack of the heuristic that required the algorithm to look at the second closest exemplar when the closest one led to an incorrect prediction. The Greedy EACH algorithm only created (or increased the size of) a hyperrectangle when it made a correct prediction. When it made an incorrect prediction, it automatically stored a new point in feature space – it did not look at the second closest match. A significant implication of this rule is that Greedy EACH *cannot* create nested hyperrectangles: recall that a rectangle is created when two points match and make the same prediction. However, a new example e_i which falls inside an existing rectangle r will always be measured closer to r than to any exception point e_j inside the rectangle, even if it is very close to e_j. The distance metric will find a small positive distance between any two points e_i and e_j, but a zero distance between a rectangle r and a point e_i within that rectangle. (It might be possible to modify the metric to allow the Greedy algorithm to find a match between e_i and e_j, but I have not experimented with such modifications.) So, although the Greedy algorithm can create exceptions – by storing points within a rectangle – it cannot created nested rectangles.

The next chapter describes the work within Artificial Intelligence that preceded my NGE learning model, and also reviews work from psychology and statistics which is directly relevant. In particular, I explain how I took the exemplar learning model recently developed in cognitive psychology and adapted it to a computational framework.

3

Review

The NGE learning model represents mainstream AI work on machine learning; that is, it is an instance of symbol processing computational models which learn to perform a task or categorize a set of objects. However, work in other fields has tackled similar problems, usually with very different techniques. Sometimes other fields use formal models quite similar to those used by researchers within AI, but generally they are very different. In this chapter, I overview work in AI, psychology, and statistics that attempts to solve the problem of learning categories or concepts. The purposes of this review are (1) to show how the exemplar-based learning theory fits into AI research, and (2) to highlight areas in which this research, other AI work, and work in related fields are complementary. Obviously, each field needs to be aware of the successes (and failures) of the others, in order to avoid re-inventing algorithms or theories that have been explored elsewhere.

3.1 Concept learning in psychology

The standard psychological paradigm for learning based on examples (or failures) is called *concept learning* or *concept identification* [Bruner, Goodnow, and Austin 1956, Posner 1973]. In concept learning experiments, of which there are many [Bourne 1966], a subject is shown, e.g., some geometrical shape or block and told that it is called a *mur* (or some other nonsense syllable) [Heidbreder 1946ab]. He is then given a number of other shapes or blocks, some of which are *murs* and some of which are not. The idea is that, by giving the subject positive and negative instances of a concept, the subject will eventually discover the correct description of that concept. Winston's program [Winston 1975] is based directly on this paradigm: the program is given a pattern of blocks, told that the pattern is called an *arch*, and then given further positive and negative instances of the pattern until it has refined the description down to exactly the right set of features. In the case of Winston's program, the problem is somewhat simplified by allowing negative instances to differ from correct examples ("hits") by only one feature (what he called a "near miss").

3.1.1 Spectator behavior

Heidbreder [1946ab] classified subjects' methods of discovering new concepts into two types of behavior, each of which is useful from the standpoint of building a functional model. The first type she called *spectator behavior*, which refers to a seemingly intuitive, passive method of identifying concepts. In spectator behavior, people observe instances of some concept, and without *consciously* forming any hypotheses, they arrive at some idea (not always correct) of what the correct concept is. The experiments often cited to demonstrate this behavior involve the use of lists of related word pairs, a relatively simple task, where the goal is to determine the relation between the words [Bouthilet 1948]. However, the same process undoubtedly accounts for much more complex hypothesis-formation behavior. Take, for example, the studies of chess by DeGroot [1965, 1966], which showed that chess masters recognize thousands of game situations that novices do not. In the course of playing many thousands of chess games, masters are constructing patterns for these game situations, storing the results, and storing variations. They build these patterns implicitly. That is, chess masters do not attempt to hypothesize that a particular pattern of pieces on the board is a good situation which they will store for later use – their acquisition of knowledge here is much more unconscious, an important characteristic of spectator behavior [Posner 1973]. So perhaps what Heidbreder called spectator behavior was really the unconscious storage and retrieval of large patterns representing situations or episodes that may be of use in later, similar situations.

3.1.2 Participant behavior

Heidbreder's other class of concept learning behavior is just the active counterpart of spectator behavior, which she calls *participant behavior*. When using this strategy, people actively (i.e., consciously) form hypotheses about the correct rules to follow and then test these hypotheses using whatever data is available (in the psychological literature, this means using the data provided by the experimenter). Philosophers and psychologists agree that people have an overwhelming desire to find some regularity in the world around them, in part because the discovery of regularities allows one to predict future events. Because one of the main goals of machine learning research is to determine how one might automatically discover regularities in the world (*hypothesis construction*) and use these regularities to modify rules (sometimes called *explanation*), the findings of psychologists about participant behavior might be especially relevant. Most of the research in the past has focussed on logical induction, following the hypothesis construction rules first described by J. S. Mill [1941] as *eliminative induction*. Mill's techniques show which hypotheses one might logically make at each step of a learning process, where the concepts to be learned are things like "a big red square," "a small, elongated rectangle," or "a blue door." Psychological experiments have focussed on the question of when people use optimal methods of narrowing down the possible hypotheses and when they do not [see, e.g., Bruner, Goodnow, and Austin 1956], but they have not attempted to study complex worlds. AI programs are now dealing with data in which discrete attributes such as color, size, and shape are too simple a description of the data, so Mill's methods, although a useful tool, are inadequate. For example, we need a theory which handles continuously valued attributes as well as discrete values.

Harking back to the discussion at the end of the first chapter, we can compare spectator and participant behavior to implicit and explicit generalization. The analogy fits very well.

3.2   Prototype theory and exemplar theory

The basis for my computational model of exemplar-based learning comes from a model created in 1978 by Medin and Schaffer, usually called the exemplar model [Medin and Schaffer 1978]. This model was developed in response to the failure of many years of experiments which attempted to confirm early models of memory and learning, the most recent (in 1978) being prototype theory [Franks and Bransford 1971, Posner and Keele 1968]. Prototypes were an improvement upon earlier models [Shepard, Hovland, and Jenkins 1961] which postulated that humans developed category descriptions which consisted of the necessary and sufficient conditions for category membership – i.e., logically valid categories. Prototypes are described by *typical*, rather than necessary and sufficient, features, which makes them more appropriate to the noisy categories typically found in the natural world. Prototype theory proposes that, for every concept that a human acquires, a prototype of that concept is created in memory. (This theory traces its roots back to ancient Greek philosophy, and Plato's notion of ideal forms, and was heavily influenced by work such as Mill's [1941], mentioned above.) Incoming perceptual signals are compared to existing prototypes to determine if they are an instance of that prototype. According to prototype theory, we have in our minds prototypes for such things as dog, cat, bird, house, and tennis racket. Experts have more finely grained prototypes, so that they can distinguish (for example) two different breeds of dog which a non-expert might not. Some early concept learning work in AI corresponds very closely to prototype theory (and was, in fact, roughly contemporary with many of the early experiments in prototype theory). For example, Winston's [1975] blocks world program learned the concept of "arch," which consisted of two blocks supporting a third block. Winston's program, in fact, learned the necessary and sufficient conditions for an arch – a notion which is more restrictive than prototypes.

Prototype theory ran into many problems, however, in the experimental literature in psychology [see, e.g., Medin and Schaffer 1978, Osherson and Smith 1981, Medin 1983]. On the one hand, it is difficult to decide just how many prototypes of a given category a person might have. Should someone have just one prototype for "dog," for example? If several prototypes are possible – for example, prototypes for "large dog," "medium dog," and "small dog" – it becomes difficult to measure people's learning rates, since different people have different categories. Moreover, it requires deciding when to make a single prototype into two; i.e., when to split categories. On the other hand, researchers have tried to determine how people can combine two separate prototypes into one; e.g., combine "pet"and "fish" to get "pet fish." [Smith and Osherson 1984]. (When asked for a typical pet fish, people give responses such as "guppy" or "goldfish"; however, when asked to name typical pets, they respond "dog" and "cat," and when asked to name typical fish they give responses such as "tuna," "bass," and "salmon." "Goldfish" is neither a prototypical pet nor a prototypical fish, yet it is a prototypical pet fish.) Furthermore, even if people have the same general categories, it is clear that individuals differ in their precise definitions of those categories, from differences in behavior on categorization tasks [e.g., Barr and Caplan 1987]. The theory of prototypes, although useful as a philosophical notion, needed modification.

Exemplar theory, as set out by Medin and Schaffer [1978], does not require people to learn (or construct) any prototypes at all. In an exemplar model of learning, every example gets stored directly in memory. Once stored in memory, it is termed an exemplar (my terminology), to distinguish it from an example. Over time, some exemplars may be forgotten, and thus the most frequently observed or distinctive exemplars will be most easily recalled. This phenomenon may lead to behavior similar to that predicted by prototype theory. Because no prototype is ever created, concepts consist of groups of similar exemplars. New examples are compared to past exemplars in order to make predictions, understand new situations, or categorize objects. For example, if a subject is asked to identify a picture of a dog, he will compare it to other dogs (or pictures of dogs) he has seen, not to a prototype "dog." Because he has seen many different sizes and shapes of dogs, he should have no more trouble identifying a large dog than a small dog. Of course, many researchers have pointed out that subjects can easily describe a "typical" dog, as well. This ability has motivated various prototype models. Exemplar models usually claim that prototypes are constructed from individual features of exemplars that have been seen many times; e.g., a subject may use his pet dog as the basis for describing a typical dog.

Exemplar theory has been successful at explaining many of the experimental results that caused prototype theory trouble, although it has not explained every empirical result. For example, although exemplar theory predicts that a subject would not prefer any exemplar when asked to describe a category, subjects generally agree on which exemplars are more "typical" than others. If asked to describe a bird, subjects will not describe a penguin or an ostrich, since these are unusual birds. Such results beg the question of whether people might still have a prototype representation of concepts. Nonetheless, subjects have no difficulty identifying penguins and ostriches as birds [Barr and Caplan 1987].

3.3   EACH as a multiple prototype model

EACH is a computational model of learning which combines features of both prototype theory and exemplar theory. It stores points initially, but allows these points to "grow" into rectangles. The resulting objects are generalizations that can also serve as prototypes. Because EACH can store multiple, distinct hyperrectangles representing the same concept, it might be described as a "multiple prototype" theory.

Suppose EACH is attempting to predict the value of a variable y whose value is dependent on the values of a set of variables $x_1, x_2, ..., x_n$. The independent variables x_i define an n-dimensional feature space, and it is this space which defines exemplar memory. Examples are stored initially in exemplar memory as points in the n-dimensional space. The seed set can be thought of as a collection of prototypes, with the important caveat that items in the seed set may have the same values of the dependent variable y, which means they describe the same category.

When processing a new example, the EACH system finds the nearest existing exemplar in feature space and predicts that the dependent variable y will have the same value for the new example as it had on the exemplar. In domains in which the prediction requires continuous output values, EACH breaks those values up into a discrete set of intervals. If the prediction is incorrect, the new example is stored as a point of its own in feature space. This new exemplar can be thought of as a new prototype. It is quite possible that the value of y stored with the new exemplar already exists on an exemplar elsewhere in feature space, which means that the system has created another prototype for the same concept. This characteristic of EACH makes it like a multiple prototype theory. It's not really a pure prototype theory, though, because they do not store exemplars. On the other hand, it's not a pure exemplar theory (as expressed in the psychology literature), because they do not allow for the generalization of exemplars.

3.4 Machine learning in AI

The area of AI known as machine learning encompasses many different kinds of work, some of which are almost completely unrelated to one another. Explanation-based generalization (EBG) was discussed earlier and will not be discussed further here, except to point out that it seems to be one of the most popular recent paradigms of machine learning work. Several other categories of machine learning work, those most closely related to exemplar-based learning, are worth mentioning in this brief review.

3.4.1   Learning by discovery

When it first appeared, Lenat's AM program [1976], which learned new
concepts in mathematical number theory simply by exploring a concept
space, was considered one of the most exciting pieces of work in the machine learning literature. The concept space was defined symbolically,
in LISP. This program discovered, seemingly on its own, such concepts
as square roots and prime numbers. After attempting to extend this
work (by building another program, Eurisko), Lenat pointed out that
AM's success was due primarily to a close correspondence between the
structure of LISP and many properties of number and set theory [Lenat
1982]. When he tried to extend the program, he found that it quickly
broke down.

Perhaps because of Lenat's success – or maybe because of his later
failure – other researchers avoided learning by discovery for a number of
years. Recently, though, work has been to sprout up in this field. Sims,
for example, has created a program called IL which explores the area
of mathematics called Conway numbers [Sims 1987]. Epstein [1987] is
working on a system which explores graph theory, by making conjectures
and attempting to prove them.

3.4.2   Natural language learning

Learning natural language has long been an important area both in natural language research and in machine learning research. The difficulty
of creating robust natural language parsers with large vocabularies has
encouraged researchers to seek automatic methods for getting language
knowledge loaded into a computer. I will not attempt to review all language learning work, but will mention two approaches that are similar
to other work on learning from examples.

Natural language understanding systems typically use grammatical
structures representing sentence and phrase types. Some use semantic
structures such as schemata representing stereotypical objects, situations, and actions [Mooney and Dejong 1985]. These schemata can be
combined to form new, more general schemata based on particular nat-

ural language stories. Mooney and Dejong give an example where their system combines a schema for bargaining with a schema for capturing and confining humans into a kidnapping schema. Martin's system [Martin and Riesbeck 1986] tries to create mappings of existing words and phrases onto new words and phrases, by looking for similarities in the surrounding sentence structure; i.e., by looking for places where a given word or phrase can be swapped for another, without changing the meaning of the sentence. Although they share with other learning programs the learning from examples approach, the representations that natural language systems manipulate are vastly different from the rules, decision trees, and structured exemplar memories of those programs.

3.4.3 Earlier work on nested generalizations

Vere's [1980] work on multilevel counterfactuals was the first and only prior work explicitly to construct a nested structure of generalizations. His system learned generalizations in the blocks world, a highly simplified domain in which the only legal relations were a few binary predicates such as (ON A B) and (BEHIND B C), and several unary predicates such as (GREEN A), (PYRAMID C), and (LARGE D).

Vere presented his program with a series of configurations of blocks, each labelled as an positive or negative example of the concept. The program produced a single description, disjunctive if necessary, that covered all positive examples and no negative examples. For example, one description produced (from [Vere 1980, p. 157]) was:

```
(ON .N1 TABLE)
 ~((ON .N5 .N3)
   ~((ON .N4 .N6)
     ~((ON .N3 TABLE)
       (ON F .N5))))
```

Adjacency in Vere's notation indicates conjunction of terms. Terms preceded by a period are variables, while other terms (F and TABLE above) are constants. The expression here is typical, according to Vere, in that it is concise (given the nature of the examples used to generate it), it contains counterfactuals (negated terms) nested several layers deep, and it is quite difficult to interpret.

Note that Vere's system worked only with symbolic features, and only with a two-category problem. It was also intolerant of noise in that the algorithm assumed the category labels were correct. However, it went considerably beyond the earlier work of Winston [1975] in that it did not require its counterexamples be "near misses"; i.e., concepts differing from the target concept in only one feature. He also showed that Winston's empirical method for deriving must-not conditions was erroneous. The importance of this work is that Vere showed that by using negated terms (his counterfactuals), one could create much more concise concept descriptions. These negated terms are conceptually similar to the exceptions created by EACH.

3.4.4 Other exemplar-based learning models

Very recently, a few researchers in AI have developed exemplar-based learning models, based, like NGE, on the exemplar model of Medin and Schaffer. The algorithms and knowledge representations used by these models differ from the NGE theory, but there are many similarities, and I will survey the domains in which these models have been applied. All of the models follow the Medin-Schaffer theory in that they store exemplars as simple points in a feature space. They also use similarity metrics, of different types, to make category decisions about new points. Unlike EACH, they do not attempt to create generalizations in the form of larger geometric objects, such as hyperrectangles. Only one of the models (Protos, see below) makes generalizations at all. They also do not subject the distance metric to a learning process, as EACH does.

Bradshaw [1987] has an exemplar based model which learns about speech sounds. The task was to recognize pronunciations of each letter of the alphabet for two different speakers; thus the prediction was a discrete value, although the features were continuous. His results were promising; in particular, his NEXUS system had an error rate of just 3%, which was seven times better than a template-matching recognition system. NEXUS stores exemplars as simple points. It does not use any weighting schemes like those described in Chapter 2, so it has no ability to adjust its distance metric. Instead, it moves points around in exemplar space by averaging them with other points (analogously to the centroid method in statistics [Everitt 1980]). Aha and Kibler [1989] call this an *instance averaging* technique.

Bareiss, Porter, and Wier [1987] have devised an exemplar-based system called Protos that uses a very different knowledge representation scheme from EACH. Their representation is in terms of conceptual categories in semantic network form, so that matching is performed in terms of the number of features matched. They do not give details of the matching, so it is not clear if they allow for weights on the features. (HANDICAPPER [Salzberg 1983, 1985], used a similar matching scheme, which counted the number of binary features matched.) Distance metrics are not relevant for their algorithm, since the features are always symbolic, as opposed to numeric values. After prediction failures, the Protos system needs a teacher to explain the correct answer. This explanation includes additional domain knowledge. Exemplars are generalized by replacing the specifications for individual features with more general specifications. For example, suppose Protos had learned the concept *chair*, with a *material* slot which was restricted to the concept *wood*. If an example of a chair came along that was made of metal, the slot's restriction would be changed to *rigid material* [ibid., p. 18]. Based on its conceptual representation and use of explanations, it can be argued that Protos is much closer to explanation-based learning programs than to EACH.

Kibler and Aha [1987] performed a comparative study of three exemplar learning algorithms, using an instance-based learning algorithm that stored examples as points. They varied their algorithm according to the suggestions of Smith and Medin [1981]: (1) the proximity algorithm stored all examples, (2) the growth algorithm incrementally stored new examples when they were incorrectly classified by the existing examples, and (3) the shrink algorithm stored all examples, and then went through them removing those that would be correctly classified by the remaining set. Both (2) and (3) are quite sensitive to the order in which the examples are processed. Kibler and Aha use Euclidean distance as their similarity metric, where values on each dimension were normalized to 1. They used data which was originally used by Quinlan and his ID3 algorithm [1986]. The data described patients with and without thyroid disease. All of Aha and Kibler's variants stored points exactly as they were in the original data, without attempting to perform generalizations.

They give results using two sets of data. On the first set, they used data with 25 attributes, some of which apparently were irrelevant (or redundant) for the classification decision. On these examples, the growth algorithm performed best at classifying patients with a hyperthyroid condition. The second set of data used only relevant attributes, where relevance was defined by those features that appeared in the decision tree generated by Quinlan on the same data. On this set, the proximity method worked best all around, but with a much larger memory requirement. In particular, it correctly classified 83% of the hyperthyroid cases and 98% of the non-hyperthyroid cases, versus 79% and 98% for the growth algorithm. However, the proximity method stored 220 exemplars (the entire data set) versus only 10 exemplars for the growth method. This dramatic difference in memory, at the cost of only a slight degradation in predictive capability, supports the argument that a modified exemplar method will provide the best trade-off between accuracy and space. If memory space is restricted, Kibler and Aha's results argue that an exemplar algorithm must find a way to avoid storing all examples.

More recently, Aha and Kibler [1989] have introduced a noise-tolerant version of their growth algorithm that outperforms their earlier programs in the presence of noise (without noise, performance is equivalent). The noise-tolerant modification essentially discards exemplars which appear to be noisy. The program determines that an exemplar is noisy by tracking its classification performance: if it makes too many misclassifications, it is assumed to be noisy. This modification, interestingly, is very similar to the weight w_H used in the EACH algorithm, which tracks the percentage of correct classifications made by each exemplar.

3.5 Connectionism

An area of machine learning research that has been especially active recently is connectionism, sometimes called "neural networks." Among the many different models have been presented in the literature, one of the most well-studied is the back propagation model of Rumelhart, Hinton, and Williams [in Rumelhart and McClelland 1986]. There have been many modifications to the back propagation algorithm which have improved its performance, as measured on certain learning tasks. As yet, there is no standard set of tasks by which to compare algorithms. However, some problems have been used particularly often as acid tests, e.g., the parity test, the XOR problem, and digit recognition.

A discussion of the basics of the connectionist architecture is beyond the scope of this book. Instead, I will briefly outline the back propagation technique and then make some comparisons with exemplar based learning.

The method of Rumelhart *et al.* for learning in a connectionist architecture is to send the input signals through a net using a "semilinear" activation function (e.g., a sigmoid).[1] Then, starting with the output layer, the back propagation algorithm revises the weights on the connections. Depending on the new weights of the output layer, it revises the layer before that, and so on backward until it reaches the input layer again.

The activation function must be non-linear and continuous so that it has a derivative, which the algorithm needs for its error correction function. This fact implies that a linear theshold unit (popular among some other connectionist researchers, in part because of its simplicity, but also because of its apparent similarity to a real neuron) will not work at all with this algorithm, since such a unit has a non-linear derivative

---

[1] Obviously, a sigmoid function is non-linear, but I will adhere to Rumelhart's use of the term semi-linear.

(infinite at the threshold and zero elsewhere). To replace the threshold, Rumelhart *et al.* use a bias measure, which behaves the same way – it's a gradual version of a threshold.

Another interesting mathematical feature of back propagation is momentum. Rumelhart, Hinton, and Williams add a momentum term to their error correction function, which effectively filters out high frequency variations in the weight space. The momentum term gives weights in the network a tendency to continue, from one cycle to the next, to change in the same direction they have been changing. This helps them travel more quickly down "ravines" in the space, a feature which gave Hinton and Sejnowski considerable trouble with the Boltzmann machine [Hinton 1981, Hinton *et al.* 1986].

Rumelhart, Hinton, and Williams claim that back propagation makes two contributions to connectionism research, one theoretical and one empirical:

1. theoretical: an efficient way of computing the derivatives of the error surface for gradient descent.

2. empirical: a demonstration that the "apparently fatal" problem of local minima is irrelevant in a wide variety of learning tasks.

The first contribution refers to the fact that most connectionist architectures essentially compute error surfaces in multi-dimensional spaces. The learning process moves the state of the system along that surface towards the smallest error (thus the term "gradient descent"). As a theoretical contribution, then, back propagation has to be viewed within the framework of other connectionist algorithms. It is difficult to compare to machine learning algorithms which are not gradient descent techniques.

On the other hand, the empirical contribution of back propagation, and of other connectionist architectures, offers several interesting points for comparison to other machine learning theories.

Back propagation is a hill-climbing method, because the error propagation function tries to reduce the difference between the desired output and the correct output at every step. Some of the earliest AI programs (most notably GPS [Ernst and Newell 1969]) used hill-climbing, but the method is often stymied by the well-known problem of local maxima (or local minima, depending on how the problem is stated). More recent work [Rose and Langley 1988] has demonstrated that hill-climbing techniques can be effective for certain machine discovery applications. The simulations of back propagation performed by Rumelhart *et al.* (discussed below) are an attempt to answer the question of how well back propagation handles this problem.

3.5.1 Simulations

Rumelhart, Hinton, and Williams ran several simulations of their machine. First, they attempted to learn the XOR problem, to answer the Minsky-Papert argument about perceptrons. (Perceptrons cannot learn to recognize an XOR pattern, where one input is on and the other is off.) The back propagation algorithm *almost* always learned it: on only 2 trials out of several hundred, it got stuck in local minima and failed to extract itself. Learning XOR successfully, in one example, took 558 sweeps through 4 input patterns. In one case where the simulation got stuck, it halted with failure after 6587 presentations of each stimulus. Based on these results, Rumelhart *et al.* claim that getting stuck is very rare.

Empirically, they are right: back propagation rarely gets stuck. However, from a more formal point of view, a problem still exists. First, if their algorithm gets stuck even rarely, then it cannot be guaranteed to learn anything. What makes the problem worse is that the machine cannot recognize that a failure has occurred: the numbers indicate that it ran 10 times longer on a failure than on a typical success before its operators realized that it was stuck and shut it down. Another issue is the number of trials it took to learn XOR. XOR is a very basic problem, and to spend 558 sweeps learning it seems unacceptable. Compared to other connectionist architectures this number does not seem too bad, and Rumelhart *et al.* do not seem to think it a problem, but compared to other learning algorithms (i.e., symbol-based procedures), it is extremely poor. Explanation-based generalization could learn XOR with just one sweep through four examples, and the same can be said of exemplar-based learning, as embodied in EACH.

Rumelhart *et al.* also ran simulations on parity, negation, binary addition, and recognition of the difference between the letter T and the letter C. For the T and C problem, for example, they re-organized the architecture of the machine so that each hidden unit was connected to a 3x3 input region (a "receptive field"), and the hidden units were arranged in a two-dimensional grid. They were able to recognize the letters in any of four orientations (normal and 90 deg, 180 deg, and 270 deg rotated).

An interesting methodological issue arises when examining these simulations: even though the back propagation algorithm is domain independent, the machine architecture was modified for each simulation, which throws the domain independence of the technique into question. Another methodological issue involves the choice of tasks. The simulations mentioned here, and many others used to test connectionist learning algorithms, run on extremely basic tasks. It would be helpful to see an argument explaining how these simple tasks could be combined to form more complex tasks. Perhaps complex tasks involve simultaneously solving hundreds or thousands of small pattern recognition tasks, in which case failure on a small percentage (as occurs with the back propagation model) might be disastrous. If, on the other hand, complex tasks can be reduced to a combination of a small number of basic tasks, maybe the connectionism may prove to be relatively robust.

This book is not the place to discuss the relative merits of one connectionist learning algorithm versus another. It is relevant, though, to point out how connectionist algorithms differ from exemplar-based learning. Most of these differences hold for explanation-based generalization and decision tree algorithms (e.g., CART – Classification and Regression Trees), as well. The biggest and most obvious distinction is in the representation of the knowledge that is learned. As I discussed in Chapter 1, inductive learning techniques create rules, decision trees, and (in the case of exemplar-based learning) structured exemplar objects. Connectionist architectures, however, create a structure *identical* to the one they start with: the only thing that changes is the weights on the connections. (One exception might be connectionist models that allow weights to change from non-zero to zero and back again. Although not true of back propagation, such a capability would be equivalent to adding and removing connections from the network.) It is therefore very difficult to identify concepts or categories that have been learned, since there are no symbols in the machine which can be identified as such. Consequently, the representation is unlikely to be meaningful to a user, even an expert in the domain, and the program must be used as a black box which produces an answer.

Another distinction between connectionism and exemplar-based learning, already mentioned above, is that connectionist architectures tend to be domain dependent, in that they need to be modified significantly for different simulations. On the other hand, the learning algorithms seem to apply across different hardware configurations, so perhaps they can be called machine independent. Considering the learning strategy dimension of Carbonell, Mitchell, and Michalski, we see that connectionist algorithms are incremental strategies, a feature they share with exemplar-based learning.

One shot learning is very difficult, and probably impossible, for a connection machine learning algorithm. Because of the gradual nature of the weight adjustment within the machine, a single example, even one very different from any seen before, cannot cause large changes in the behavior of the machine. Typically we find that connection machines require thousands of iterations to define a concept, rather than just one. It is conceivable, though, that if an example represented a completely new category (as opposed to an unknown example of an existing category), then a connectionist algorithm might be devised which could respond to this example.

3.6   Cluster analysis

There is a family of statistical techniques known as *cluster analysis*
which, although not designed for learning, perform classification tasks
very similar to those performed by inductive learning methods in AI.
The general goal of cluster analysis is to take a set of measurements,
each representing one example, and group them into *clusters*, where
the intra-cluster similarity is much greater than inter-cluster similarity.
The majority of cluster analysis techniques focus on a similarity matrix
which contains measurements of the similarity between every pair of
data points [Everitt 1980]. The computation of this similarity matrix is
one of the main sources of differences among cluster analysis algorithms.
I will outline a few similarity metrics here, and point out which ones
are most similar to the exemplar learning model.

3.6.1   Similarity measures

For binary variables, there are quite a few different measures of the
similarity between two individuals. The obvious measure is to give a
match a score of 1 if the two individuals have the same value for a given
variable, and a 0 otherwise. More generally, though, for two examples
x_1, x_2 we can take counts a, b, c, and d of the four possible ways they
might match on a given binary variable:[2]

$$
\begin{array}{c|cc}
 & \multicolumn{2}{c}{x_2} \\
 & + & - \\
\hline
x_1 \quad + & a & b \\
- & c & d \\
\end{array}
$$

For instance, if both examples have a positive value for three binary
variables, then $a = 3$. If x_1 is positive and x_2 is negative for two
variables, then $b = 2$.

Now, to score the match between x_1 and x_2, we need to combine the
scores a, b, c, d for the two examples. Here is where all the differences

---

[2]from Everitt [1980], p. 12

in scoring techniques arise; for example, many choose to ignore negative matches (d in the above table). Some add an additional variable p, where $p = a + b + c + d$ (p is also a count of the total number of variables). In general, the individual researcher decides on a particular metric based on his own familiarity with the data, but the most common are:[3]

$$\frac{a+d}{p},$$

$$\frac{a}{a+b+c},$$

$$\frac{a}{p},$$

$$\frac{2a}{2a+b+c},$$

$$\frac{2(a+d)}{2(a+d)+b+c}, \text{ and}$$

$$\frac{a}{a+2(b+c)}.$$

Differences among these equations include those that give matched pairs of variables twice the weight of unmatched pairs (a heuristic used by HANDICAPPER [Salzberg 1985]), those that ignore negative matches, and those that ignore mismatches (the b and c variables).

For continuous variables, cluster analysis requires the construction of *distance metrics* to measure similarity, viewing the two examples as points in Euclidean n-dimensional space, E^n. Here is where we find the greatest commonality between cluster analysis and the EACH exemplar-based learning model. The obvious distance metric to use, and the most commonly used one among cluster analysis methods, is simple Euclidean distance, d_{xy}, defined as:

$$d_{xy} = \sqrt{\sum_{i=1}^{m}(x_i - y_i)^2}$$

---

[3] ibid., p. 13

where d_{xy} is the distance between individuals x and y, and x_i is the value of the ith variable on x. Euclidean distance has the flaw that it is badly affected by the scale of the variables, so it is usually scaled in some way, typically by dividing each x_i by σ_i, where σ_i is the standard deviation of the ith variable.

Changing the exponents in the above metric (one exponent is 2, and the other is 1/2), produces a family of distance metrics called the Minkowski metrics. The most common of these, besides the Euclidean metric, is the *city block metric*. In the city block metric, both exponents (the square root and the square terms) are set to one. This metric is typically used when the variables are known to be independent of one another. Higher-order metrics, with the exponents set to n and $1/n, n >$ 2, are possible but not used in any common clustering algorithms.

3.6.2   Hierarchical clustering techniques

There are two basic types of hierarchical clustering techniques, which are essentially mirror images of each other. *Divisive* techniques start by treating the entire data set as one big cluster, which they gradually split into many smaller clusters. This tactic is similar to the way Quinlan's ID3 creates decision trees, and like Quinlan's is a non-incremental approach. In fact, many of the problems of divisive techniques are precisely those described by Quinlan [1986]; for example, the problem of deciding what attribute to split on, and the problem of deciding when to stop splitting. *Agglomerative* techniques start by treating every data point as a separate cluster and gradually combining these into larger clusters. Agglomeration is closer to generalized exemplar-based learning in spirit, since the latter also combines objects in feature space to create larger objects.

There are a variety of ways of determining how similar two clusters are to one another. The *nearest neighbor* method chooses the two points in clusters C1 and C2 which are closest to each other; i.e., there is no other pair of points, one in C1 and one in C2, which are closer [McQuitty 1957, Cover and Hart 1967]. The *centroid* method [Sokal and

Michener 1958] replaces pairs of clusters, when they are fused together, by the coordinates of their centroids. The distance between groups is simply the distance between these centroid points, and those groups closest together are fused first. (This is an agglomerative method.) The disadvantage of this method is that if the sizes of the two groups to be fused are very different, then the new centroid will be biased towards the larger group. *Median cluster analysis* assumes that groups are the same size, and thus puts the new centroid between two groups being fused. The *group average* method defines the distance between two clusters as the average distance between all pairs of individuals in two groups. There are many other methods, but even this very short list illustrates the diversity of possibilities.

The most common applications of these techniques have been in the biological sciences, where they are used for taxonomic tasks. For example, cluster analysis has been used to investigate plant communities [Pritchard and Anderson 1971], where the task is to divide a natural environment into sub-environments (defined as physical regions). Cluster analysis has been used for other kinds of problems, too; for example, Wishart [1969] has applied cluster analysis to geology.

All of the above techniques produce distinct clusters, but there is another set of techniques, known as *clumping* techniques, which allows overlapping clusters. It is interesting to note that these were first introduced by language researchers [Needham 1967]. Linguistic classes, apparently, tend to require overlapping definitions.

3.6.3 Problems with cluster analysis

Normally we think of clusters as regions of relatively high density in feature space, where the inter-cluster density is much lower than intra-cluster density. These *natural clusters* can take any shape at all: convex, concave, irregular, elongated, and so on. However, almost every clustering technique finds clusters of a particular shape; e.g., spherical, "which implies that we are interested in finding spherical homogenous clusters, and clusters of this shape will be found even if the natural clusters in the data are of other shapes" [Everitt 1980, p. 69]. If the clusters in a given data set do not fit the shape for which the technique is best suited, it may not find the right clusters. Some agglomerative algorithms have been devised which avoid this problem by including points in a cluster C which are within a constant distance from *any* point in C, but these algorithms have difficulty separating two clusters that are connected by a "bridge" of points, even though the bridge might represent noise.

Exemplar based learning (as implemented in EACH, at least), shows a similar preference for a particular shape (actually, a class of shapes, which I have called hyperrectangles), but this bias is weakened considerably by the mechanism for storing exceptions. Since exceptions can be stored anywhere inside a hyperrectangle, EACH is not restricted to convex solids: the objects in its memory may have many "holes" in them defined by exceptions. Furthermore, since multiple hyperrectangles can be used for a single concept, any shape can be approximated by a sufficient number of adjacent exemplars.

Another problem with clustering techniques is deciding how many clusters to create (this is analogous to the problem of deciding when to stop splitting when creating decision trees). Most of the solutions to this problem employ scoring heuristics which indicate when the algorithm should stop splitting the data into additional clusters. This problem is still open, though, as pointed out by Everitt:

> Overall, the problem of determining the most appropriate number of clusters for a set of data can be a difficult one. Despite the numerous attacks on the problem in the literature it must be said that no completely satisfactory solution is available.... Perhaps the problem is in fact *incapable* of any formal solution in a truly general sense simply because there is no universally acceptable definition of the term cluster. [p. 66]

There are additional problems with specific methods; for example, the nearest neighbor technique may fail to separate clusters if a small number of intermediate points (a "chain") connects them. Hierarchical techniques have difficulty if they mis-allocate points early on, since backup is not usually allowed (and would be very expensive). Cluster analysis research is currently addressing many of these problems, at the same time that researchers in AI and in statistics are beginning to share techniques and ideas. For example, Kibler and Aha [1987] have adapted cluster analysis to their instance-based learning work. Quinlan [1986] and Breiman et al. [1984] have developed distinct methods for creating decision trees, one based on information theory and the other on statistics.

3.7 Conclusion

This review has covered areas of AI, psychology, and statistics which are closely related to the exemplar-based learning model. There is, of course, other related work in all of these fields, both on concept learning and on other forms of learning. What this brief review was intended to show, though, was how all three fields are investigating essentially the same problem, albeit with different methodologies and slightly different goals. Outstanding problems at the moment are: (1) determining the number of categories automatically, (2) dealing with noisy or incomplete data, and (3) reconciling the use of prototypes with specific exemplar models. EACH offers answers to each of these problems.

In the context of previous AI work, especially that on machine learning, exemplar-based learning represents a break from the mainstream work. Machine learning research in AI has taken two parallel paths, which might be termed the context dependent path and the context free path, to borrow terms from computational linguistics. Explanation-based learning is context dependent, because it requires the machine to acquire and use domain knowledge as part of the learning process. In fact, one of the tenets of explanation-based learning is that domain knowledge is essential for the creation of explanations, and explanations in turn are an important component of learning. Exemplar-based learning follows the context free path in machine learning (as does connectionism), in that it requires no domain knowledge, with the resulting advantage that the exemplar algorithm can be applied (as shown in Chapter 4) to many different domains with virtually no changes. On the other hand, context dependent theories can build up a base of domain specific knowledge that might not be discovered with other models. As both branches of machine learning progress, it should become possible to combine them, so that a single system can first identify the relevant features and background knowledge for a complex domain, and then begin acquiring predictive knowledge in that domain using an model – such as the NGE learning theory – which is applicable to many other learning domains.

4

Experimental results with NGE

The EACH program has been tested in several domains, using two different configurations of the program. The results presented below used four different problems: (1) predicting the recurrence of breast cancer, (2) classifying iris flowers, (3) predicting survival for heart attack victims, and (4) predicting the dependent variable in a discrete event simulation. The simulation problem was based on a very simplified stock market model. In the process of testing EACH on these problems, the algorithm has been tuned in various ways, and much has been learned about the kinds of problems on which EACH performs well, and those on which it performs poorly. In particular, in the test runs for the simulation, I was able to vary such things as the number of variables and the complexity of the underlying relationships quite freely. For the real data used in the other sets of test runs, the variables were fixed. Thus the simulation allowed me to test the system in a more controlled way, while the real data offered a chance to test the system with data which was in some cases very noisy and incomplete, and, most importantly, to compare EACH with other systems.

Below, I briefly explain each data set (or simulation), and then present the results. The main results are (1) summaries of EACH's learning rate and peak performance rate, (2) summaries of the memory requirements, and (3) comparisons. *Learning rate* is simply the rate at which the system's performance changes, and *peak performance rate* is the maximum performance level of the system, measured as the percentage of correct predictions or classifications. Comparisons are made between EACH and other learning models on the three sets of real data. Different experimental designs were required in order to compare EACH to previously published results, since the previous work (by different authors) used differing methodologies. Only by replicating those methodologies as closely as possible could I make valid comparisons. Thus, if an earlier experiment used four randomized presentations of the training set, I also used four. For the simulated data the experimental methodology is my own, since that data was not used in any previously published work.

4.1   Breast cancer data

The first problem domain for EACH was predicting the recurrence of breast cancer. The examples consisted of 273 patients who underwent surgery to remove tumors, all of whom were followed up five years later.[1] The task given to EACH was to predict whether or not breast cancer would recur during that five year period. Nine variables were measured, three binary and six either real-valued or discrete. The binary variables included whether or not the patient had been through menopause, which breast had had cancer, and whether or not radiation treatment had been used. The real valued and discrete variables included the age of the patient, the diameter of the tumor in millimeters, and several other measures of the tumor itself. The dependent variable was binary: the prediction was either T, meaning the patient did suffer a recurrence of cancer, or NIL, meaning she did not.

This data set is identical to that used by Michalski, Mozetic, Hong, and Lavrac [1986] in a study of the incremental learning algorithm AQ15. I present a comparison of EACH's results with AQ15's results in the discussion below. AQ15 is a rule learning program which uses

---

[1] Stuart Crawford of Advanced Decision Systems provided this data.

a logic-based rule language to represent the rules it learns. Thus the representations learned by AQ15 and EACH are completely different.

To make a proper comparison, I use the same testing methodology used by Michalski *et al.* For each trial, the examples were divided into a training set and a test set. Seventy percent of the examples were randomly chosen for each trial to be in the training set. Four different trials were run, and the final results are an average of those trials.

In order to make a comparison to human performance, Michalski *et al.* tested five human experts on the same examples. The human prognoses were correct in 64% of the cases. Michalski *et al.* report that random guessing would produce 50% correct. However, it would be unfair not to note that approximately 70% of the patients fell into the non-recurrence category. Hence a strategy of predicting NIL for every example would give a 70% success rate, although it would be incorrect for 100% of the cases in which T was the right response. One must assume that Michalski used a strategy of randomly choosing T or NIL to produce the 50% figure.

4.1.1 Success rates and comparisons

The best performance of EACH came with $\Delta_f = 0.05$, where it did considerably better than above: its success rate was 78%. Table 4.1 gives a summary of EACH's performance on this data set with different values of Δ_f. The same data is shown graphically in Figure 4.1. AQ15 had success rates of 66%, 66%, and 68%, using three different configurations of that program. Taking 68% as the performance rate of AQ15, a t test on EACH's success rate finds that EACH is significantly better, $p <$ .01, than AQ15. The improvement over human experts is even more marked. Without using the feature adjustment rate; i.e., setting $\Delta_f = 0$, EACH's success rate on the training sets was 69%, approximately equal to the performance of AQ15. This latter result shows that adjusting the weights w_i on features produced a significantly more accurate model.

Δ_f	Success rate (%)
0.00	69
0.02	73
0.05	78
0.10	73
AQ15	68
Doctors	64

Table 4.1: Success rates for different settings of Δ_f.

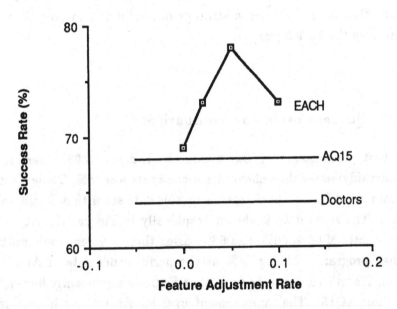

Figure 4.1: Relative classification performance on breast cancer data.

Trial	Success rate (%)	Memory Size
I	78	29
II	82	30
III	79	24
IV	72	32
Average	78	29

Table 4.2: Variability in success rate for $\Delta_f = 0.05$.

4.1.2 Variability

To give a measure of EACH's sensitivity to the order of the inputs, I looked at the variability across the four test runs when Δ_f was 0.05. It varied significantly, but not terribly so, from a low of 72% to a high of 82%, as shown in Table 4.2. However, even the lowest of these numbers surpasses both the expert performance rate and AQ15. Numbers on the variance of AQ15 with the different orders of its inputs were not available.

4.1.3 Memory size

The average size of memory after processing the entire data set of 273 patients was just 29 exemplars. This number ranged from a low of 24 to a high of 32, as shown in Table 4.2. This results supports the claim that exemplar-based learning – in particular, the NGE learning model – produces a model of the domain which is not only accurate, but also quite compact. Table 4.2 also shows that the largest memory corresponded to the lowest success rate. This correspondence is not accidental, since the NGE model stores new exemplars in memory only when it makes mistakes. If the error rate is high, therefore, the program will create more exemplars.

4.1.4 Other tests

Some interesting properties of the algorithm were observed in other tests using the same data. In particular, the effect of the feature adjustment rate, Δ_f, on the learning rate was very good as long as Δ_f was kept small. With $\Delta_f = 0.02$, for example, the success rate was 75%, still a very good result. If Δ_f grew too large, though, the weight adjustments eventually got out of hand, cancelling the effects of earlier weight adjustments and biasing the overall model in the wrong direction. With $\Delta_f = 0.10$, the over-adjustment effect was small, but beginning to be noticeable – the system performed at a 72% success rate, better than with $\Delta_f = 0$, but not as well as with $\Delta_f = 0.05$. These results are shown in Table 4.1. Similar effects were noted in tests on different data sets, as will be shown later in this chapter.

One final note: a pattern not evident from any of the results above is that there seemed to be a few particularly difficult examples in the data set. These examples fell into sparsely populated areas of feature space. As one would expect, if these difficult examples happened to fall in the training set, the program would do less well during training but would do better on the test set. On the other hand, if the difficult examples occurred in the test set, EACH's performance on that set would suffer.

4.2   Iris classification

The next task given to EACH was that of classifying a set of 150 iris flowers, using a data set from [Fisher 1936].[2] Each of the examples consists of four integer-valued variables – making it the smallest vector used in the tests of EACH – plus a known assignment of the example to a particular species of iris. The data covered three different species: *I. virginica*, *I. setosa*, and *I. versicolor*. The four variables measured were sepal length, sepal width, petal length, and petal width. The ranges of these variables were 43-79, 20-44, 10-56, and 1-24 respectively, although EACH was not given these ranges ahead of time. This well-known data set has been used for many previous experiments, and it has the characteristic that two of the three categories of data are not linearly separable.

---

[2]Stuart Crawford provided machine readable data for this task.

Δ_f	Success rate (%)	Memory size
0.00	93	5
0.05	92	5
0.25	88	12
0.00 (pre-set weights)	95	5

Table 4.3: Success rates for iris flowers at different values of Δ_f.

4.2.1   Success rates

For each of the tests reported below, EACH used a seed set of five exemplars. Thus the test results report EACH's success rates (or, conversely, its error rates) for 145 examples.

With feature adjustment rate = 0, EACH made 135 correct classifications, for a success rate of 93%, which is equivalent to an error rate of 7%. With feature adjustment set to 0.05, EACH performed approximately the same, getting 134 classifications correct, for a success rate of 92%. These error rates are summarized in Table 4.3.

We can notice immediately that these success rates are large compared to the success rate for the breast cancer data, indicating that the four variables used were good discriminators for the three categories. Note that with Δ_f set to 0.25 (the largest value I tried), performance was noticeably poorer. This performance drop-off at high values of Δ_f occurred in the previous experiment, too. As mentioned earlier, rapid adjustment of the feature weights results in over-corrections, which causes poor performance.

The weights which EACH assigned to the four variables in the trial where $\Delta_f = 0.05$ were 1.0, 1.05, 2.08, and 2.18, to sepal length, sepal width, petal length, and petal width, respectively. In an additional experiment, I pre-set the feature weights to the weights learned above, and found that EACH then scored 138 successes, for an success rate of 95%. This result also appears in Table 4.3. My conclusion from this test was that the weights learned in the initial run were an important part of the resulting model of the domain, even though performance with

Trial	Success rate (%)	Memory size
I	93	5
II	92	6
III	93	6
IV	88	8
V	94	9
VI	94	7
Average	92.4	6.8

Table 4.4: Memory requirements rates for iris flowers, $\Delta_f = 0$.

$\Delta_f = 0$ was excellent for these 145 examples. If a larger data set were available, the weighted distance metric learned by EACH possibly would outperform the unweighted metric. This result using pre-set weights suggests that Δ_f should be set to a positive value for some fixed number of examples at the beginning of learning trials, and perhaps set to zero thereafter (or reduced gradually).

One more result of interest is the *post hoc* success rate, which was 95%. This result and others are reported in Table 4.5, which compares EACH with another version of itself and with a decision tree program (CART), both discussed below. The *post hoc* rate shows how well the five exemplars from the trial with $\Delta_f = 0$ fit the data used to create those exemplars. The exemplars (shown graphically below) correctly classify 143 of the 150 examples in the data set.

4.2.2   Memory size and variability

Another very important measure of the algorithm's success is how many exemplars it stored in memory. In every case, this number was quite small – in the first two trials in Table 4.3, EACH only needed the five seeds as the basis of its exemplars. To give a better idea of the memory requirements, I ran five more trials, all with $\Delta_f = 0$, and counted the number of exemplars in memory for each trial. These results, plus the first trial reported above, are reported in Table 4.4. The table shows that the largest memory created contained only nine exemplars. This

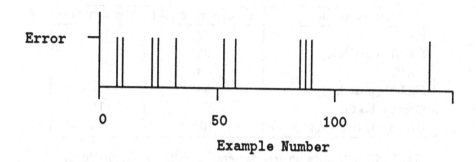

Figure 4.2: Sequence of errors on iris categorization task.

compactness is a nice advantage of NGE over other models, including other exemplar-based learning models. Some instance-based learning models, in particular, store every single example (Kibler and Aha [1987] use such models as a basis for comparison to their own exemplar-based models), and these require much more memory than NGE.

4.2.3 Learning rate

Let's go back and look again at the trial in which $\Delta_f = 0.05$, and examine EACH's learning rate. If we consider the first 2/3 of the data (96 examples) as a training set, and the last 1/3 (49 examples) as the test set, then we find that EACH improves over time: for the training set in the first trial, the success rate was 90%, while for the test set, the success rate was 98%. Figure 4.2 illustrates this learning rate. The vertical lines in the figure show exactly where EACH made mistakes in its run through 145 examples. Thus, although its success rate is close to 100% in the beginning, it gets even closer with experience.

4.2.4 Comparisons

Crawford [1988] used the same data set for one of his experiments with a decision tree learning system. He reports an estimated error rate (using a cross validation technique, which replaces the use of a separate test data set) of 7% for an incremental version of the CART (Classification

Program or version	Success rate (%)	Memory size
EACH	93	5
EACH (post hoc)	95	5
CART	93	–
CART (post hoc)	96	–
Greedy EACH	90	16
Greedy EACH (post hoc)	100	16

Table 4.5: Results on iris flowers for different algorithms.

And Regression Trees) algorithm, which creates decision trees. This rate corresponds to a 93% success rate, which for all practical purposes is identical to the rate reported here for the EACH algorithm. I include this result in Table 4.5 as the CART success rate. Crawford also reports a "resubstitution" error rate of 4%, which is the rate obtained by classifying data with the same tree generated from that data. This corresponds to a 96% success rate, and is entered in Table 4.5 as the CART *post hoc* rate. It is rougly equal to the 95% *post hoc* success rate achieved by EACH. Thus the exemplar-based algorithm performs approximately the same as a decision tree algorithm on this data set.

It should be noted that Crawford's research compares an incremental CART algorithm to standard CART, which is non-incremental. Quinlan's ID3 algorithm, another decision tree learning system, is also non-incremental. Both algorithms in Crawford's study had similar error rates. Crawford's goal was to create an incremental version of CART without incurring significant additional computational cost, and he seems to have had some success.

4.2.5 Memory size and structure

Perhaps the most interesting feature of the model learned by EACH in this iris classification task is that it needed very few exemplars to achieve its performance. On one trial, it needed only the five exemplars used as the seed set. This is a remarkably small memory model, given its excellent success rate. Of those five exemplars, three were used

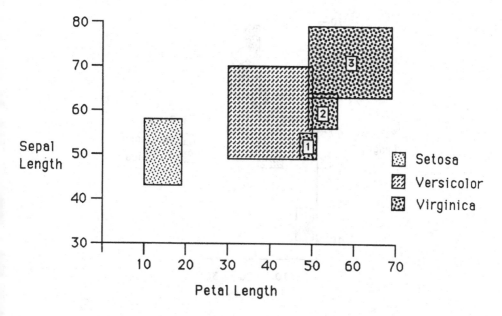

Figure 4.3: Sepal length vs. petal length for iris flowers.

for the category *I. virginica*, and only one for each of the other two categories, indicating that *virginica* was the most difficult category to define. Although it is impossible to show the hyperrectangles in four dimensions, they can be shown two dimensions at a time. Figures 4.3 through 4.5 show three two-dimensional views of the rectangles. Since three of the rectangles correspond to the same category, *I. Virginica*, numbers are used in the figures to identify the exemplars. Thus the rectangle marked 1 in Figure 4.3 is the same exemplar as that marked 1 in Figure 4.5. These three graphs illustrate three of the six possible pairs of relationships among the four variables.

One final note here is that, as with the echocardiogram data presented below, it is possible to create a model which gives a perfect *post hoc* success rate – that is, it makes zero errors – by using the Greedy EACH algorithm. The model created with Greedy EACH used 16 exemplars, instead of just five, and it achieved a perfect (100%) *post hoc* fit to the data, as opposed to the 95% *post hoc* figure reported above (see

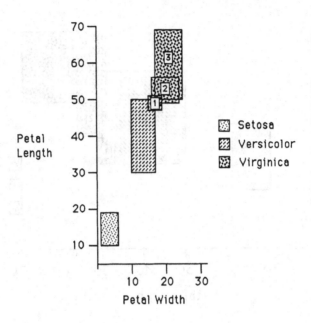

Figure 4.4: Petal length vs. petal width for iris flowers.

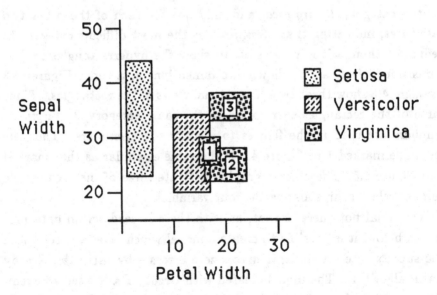

Figure 4.5: Sepal width vs. petal width for iris flowers.

Table 4.5). In addition, it reached its final state after 90 examples, and it made no mistakes, even on the first run through the data, after that. It made more mistakes than the original model, however, on the first 90 examples – 14 errors as opposed to 9. Thus its success rate for the training set (the first 2/3 of the data, 96 examples) was low, 85%, but its error rate on the test set was 0%. Recall that the success rate for the training set using the original EACH algorithm was 90%, and the success rate on the test set was 98%. A conclusion to be reached from this result is that, if memory size is not a problem (normally the case for small data sets), the Greedy EACH learning algorithm might work best. On the other hand, with large data sets, the Greedy EACH algorithm may cause memory to grow too fast.

4.3 Echocardiogram tests

The last set of real data used as a test of the EACH program was from a set of people who had recently suffered acute myocardial infarctions; i.e., heart attacks. This data set is the smallest of the four presented in this chapter, but the difficulties it presented allowed me to explore other aspects of the learning model. It also provided an opportunity to compare EACH to another data modelling technique, one used by medical researchers on the same data. In addition to being noisy these data were incomplete in the sense that more variables seem necessary in order to consistently classify the patients.

4.3.1 Description of the domain

First, I will briefly describe the data set, to provide a context for the analysis which follows. Each example is a record for one patient. All patients had heart attacks, so there is no need for a variable indicating this fact. The data includes several measures taken from echocardiograms, which are ultrasound measurements of the heart itself. The goal of physicians using these measurements is to be able to predict a patient's chances of survival. In particular, experimental work is being performed currently to determine if an echocardiogram (in conjunction with other measures) can be used to predict whether or not a patient will survive longer than a certain time period; e.g., one year. A non-invasive procedure such as an echocardiogram is clearly preferable (being much less painful than other techniques) for prognoses of heart attack victims, if it is possible to make accurate predictions. The data used in these trials were provided by a medical researcher (E. Kinney) who is using a statistical regression model (Cox regression) to predict whether patients will live beyond one year after a heart attack [Kinney 1988]. In addition, an earlier study [Kan *et al.* 1986] used echocardiograms to predict the same variable, with similar results. (Kan's study used a different data set, containing 345 patients.)

The variables used by Kinney [1988] and by EACH are described below. It should be noted that the patients were followed for a considerable time after taking the echocardiogram measurements, in order for the variables on survival to be recorded.

still-alive. A binary variable, where 0 means dead at end of one year, and 1 means still alive. This was the dependent variable.

age-at-heart-attack. Age in years when heart attack occurred.

pericardial-effusion. A binary variable. Pericardial effusion is fluid around the heart. 0 = no fluid, 1 = fluid.

fractional-shortening. A measure of contractility around the heart, where lower numbers are increasingly abnormal.

E-point septal separation. Another measure of contractility, where larger numbers are increasingly abnormal.

left ventricular end-diastolic dimension. This is a measure of the size of the heart at end-diastole. Large hearts tend to be sick hearts.

wall-motion-score. A measure of how the segments of the left ventricle are moving. For more details see [Kan *et al.* 1986].

wall-motion-index. Equal to wall-motion-score divided by the number of segments seen. Usually 12-13 segments are seen in an echocardiogram.

A quick count shows eight variables in the above list, one of which (survival) is the variable we want to predict; however, wall motion score was not used because wall motion index provided a better measure of the same variable.

Because the prediction was binary, there are two results to report: positive predictive accuracy and negative predictive accuracy. These are defined as follows: for each of the two predictions, EACH's prediction can be either right or wrong (a "success" or a "failure"). The four cases are named as follows: a "positive success" is when the program correctly predicted the patient would live. A "positive failure" is when the program incorrectly predicted the patient would live. A "negative success" is when EACH correctly predicted the patient would die. A "negative failure" is when the program incorrectly predicted the patient would die. The most interesting results concern negative successes, because it is with these that doctors have the most difficulty. The best statistical models are only correct about 60% of the time in predicting that a patient will die [Kan *et al.* 1986, Kinney 1988]. This figure is called the *negative predictive accuracy*, and more discussion of it appears below. The accuracy of a model at predicting that a patient will live is the *positive predictive accuracy.* My hope was that EACH could match the results of the statistical models of Kan and Kinney. If so, I also wanted it to do so with relatively small memory models. The tables below show results for different runs of EACH on the same data, where EACH was set up differently (as explained before each trial) on those different trials.

4.3.2 Results and discussion

The data in the tests below include 119 patients. Of these, just three were sufficient as a seed set, leaving 116 patients for the learning trials.[3]

---

[3]Thanks to Dr. Evlin Kinney of The Reed Institute, Miami, Florida, for collecting and providing me with the data. Some of the trials used slightly fewer patients

The tables below show trials in pairs: the first line of each table shows how the system performed on its very first pass through the data, while the second line shows how well the system performed after seeing the data one or more times. This second line, then, is a *post hoc* measure of how well the model created by the system fits the data: it is analogous to a correlation coefficient. The reason for presenting such a result is to compare it to the results presented in *Kan et al.* [1986], who give measures of how well their statistical model fits the patient database used to create it. I give the Kan study results in the same tables – but note that this study used a different data set. Unfortunately, they did not then apply their model to a new set of patients to see how well it could predict their survival rates. Thus their model only gives a *post hoc* fit to the data. For the purposes of comparison, therefore, I use the EACH *post hoc* results. Comparisons of predictive performance cannot be made without additional data. However, EACH makes predictions on every example the very first time it sees it, so I present EACH's predictive performance as well as its *post hoc* accuracy at fitting a model to the training sets. (The success rates I report for EACH on its initial runs through the data are not truly comparable to any measures made using statistical techniques, because those techniques do not learn incrementally. This kind of measure is appropriate for comparison only with other incremental learning programs.)

Of course, a better confirmation of the models created by EACH and by *Kan et al.* [1986] would be given by comparing their predictions on new sets of data, but additional data was not available. The small size of the data set used for these test made the obvious strategy of dividing the data in half unfeasible. Table 4.6 shows the first run of EACH on the data. This and subsequent tables report both negative predictive accuracy — the percentage of correct negative predictions — and positive predictive accuracy — the percentage of correct positive predictions. Negative predictive accuracy here is 56%, based on 18 negative predictions, of which 10 were correct. The total size of memory – the number

---

because Dr. Kinney was still collecting data while I was running the trials.

	Negative accuracy (%)	Positive accuracy (%)	Overall accuracy (%)	Size of memory
EACH (1st run)	56	79	75	11
EACH (post hoc)	90	96	94	29
Kinney	60	–	–	–
Kan et al.	61	97	86	–

Table 4.6: Echocardiogram success rates.

of exemplars stored by the system to achieve this performance – was 11. This is a surprisingly compact model.

A subsequent run of the system, in which it has seen all the examples before, shows that with more exemplars it can build a much more accurate model. (Running the data through the system several times mimics the techniques used by non-incremental algorithms.) This result also appears in table 4.6. Now the negative predictive accuracy is 90%, far better than the model in [Kan *et al.* 1986], which reported a negative predictive accuracy of 61%. Cox regression on the same data as that used here gives a negative predictive accuracy of 60% [Kinney 1988]. (Again, note that these numbers represent *post hoc* fits to the data.) The size of memory constructed by EACH to achieve this level of accuracy was 29 exemplars. Thus 29 objects were used to model the behavior of 119 objects, with excellent results, as overall the system was correct on 94% of its predictions.

4.3.3 Structure of memory model

One useful feature of exemplar based learning is that the user can examine the memory after learning, and glean some useful information from it. The model of these heart patients with 19 objects has the following characteristics: five of the exemplars carry the prediction T, meaning that the patient will survive beyond one year. As most of the patients do live more than a year, we expect these five hyperrectangles to be quite large. In fact, they are very large, and the largest one covers 25%

```
f1:  Age at time of heart attack: (62 85)
f2:  Pericardial effusion: T
f3:  Fractional shortening (0.07 0.26)
f4:  E-point septal separation (8.5 20)
f5:  Left ventricular end-diastolic dimension (4.65 5.47)
f6:  Wall motion index (1.38 2.25)
Prediction: NIL
Weight: .556
```

Figure 4.6: Exemplar created from echocardiogram data.

of the entire feature space. This is akin to a default prediction of T, which is the correct default for this domain.

Because the prediction of NIL (that the patient will die within a year) is more difficult to make correctly, it is expected that the system will create more objects in order to capture the various generalizations that indicate a NIL outcome. Thus 14 objects predict NIL. Of these, seven are simple points; i.e., they were never made into hyperrectangles. Each of the other seven points was used successfully in a prediction, and thus was expanded into a hyperrectangle. Thus the generalization that the system learned can be considered a disjunct of these fourteen exemplars (seven points and seven hyperrectangles), where each exemplar can be considered a conjunction of all the input variables. These exemplars can then be given to doctors as descriptions of patients who are unlikely to survive longer than one year, or they could be used as the basis of further data collection. For example, Figure 4.6 shows an exemplar created by EACH that predicts that the patient will not survive beyond one year. This exemplar says that if the patient's age is between 62 and 85, and pericardial effusion exists, and the other variables fall into the ranges shown, then the prediction is that the patient will die within one year. The weight indicates that this exemplar has made correct predictions in 55.6% of the cases in which it has been used (it was used nine times, and was correct on five of those uses). This exemplar is a relatively good predictor, since only about 20% of all heart attack

	Negative accuracy (%)	Positive accuracy (%)	Overall accuracy (%)	Size of memory
Greedy (1st run)	56	80	78	28
Greedy (post hoc)	100	100	100	28
Kan et al.	61	97	86	–

Table 4.7: Results from Greedy algorithm.

patients die within a year.

4.3.4 Greedy EACH algorithm results

A natural question to ask about the echocardiogram results is, why is it not possible to get the exemplar model to fit the data perfectly; i.e., why are there still some examples that the system cannot predict correctly? Well, in fact the exemplar model could almost always be guaranteed to fit the data perfectly, using a trivial model: if the system stored every example verbatim, it would match most data perfectly. The only time it would make a mistake would be when two identical inputs had different outcomes. With this model, however, the system would have failed to create any useful generalizations.

The results of using the Greedy EACH algorithm on the echocardiogram data were impressive: on its first run through the data, Greedy EACH's performance is comparable to the performance of the original algorithm. But after running the data through again, we find that the system has created a perfect model – it gets every prediction right – and the memory still only contains 28 exemplars. These results are shown in Table 4.7. Negative predictive accuracy in Table 4.7 is 56%, just as it was for the original EACH algorithm. This value is based on 9 negative predictions, of which 5 were correct (the original EACH algorithm made 18 negative predictions, of which 10 were correct). More important, memory contains just 28 exemplars. Recall that the original algorithm only created 11 exemplars on its first pass through the data, but used 29 to achieve its 90% negative predictive accuracy. Greedy

EACH created *zero* new exemplars on its second pass through the data, since its model was predicting perfectly. Of course, one could argue that the system should predict the data perfectly, since it has seen it all already (modulo genuinely inconsistent outcomes), but remember that the model created by the system contains far fewer data points than the complete set of examples.

The memory was again structured as a few large hyperrectangles that predicted NIL, and many smaller rectangles that predicted T. The conclusion from these trials is that the "second chance" heuristic that tries to conserve memory did not provide a significant advantage in this domain. This does not mean that the heuristic never works, but it indicates that it should be used with care. As reported earlier in this chapter, the Greedy EACH algorithm was applied to the iris data with mixed results. It created a *post hoc* model which was larger (16 exemplars versus 5) but more accurate (100% versus 95%). However, on the first pass through the data, the Greedy algorithm did not perform as well as the original algorithm, which indicates that the original algorithm is superior at prediction of new examples. The original algorithm also has the capability of nesting hyperrectangles, which the Greedy algorithm cannot do.

4.4   Discrete event simulation

Although it is presented last here, the discrete event simulation was used as the very first test in the evolution of EACH as a research program. The simulation was designed with a mixture of independent and interdependent variables, and was structured so that variables could easily be added and removed from the model. It was based on a greatly simplified model of a stock market. The simulation had discrete cycles, in which every variable changed according to a set of simulation equations. The variable that EACH was trying to predict was called "price," and was intended to reflect the future price of a stock in the simulated market environment.

The main purpose of the simulation was to test the sensitivity of

EACH to the feature adjustment rate (Δ_f), the number of features, and the number of categories (measured by the number of possible values of the output). EACH was able to achieve good performance in most tests where there was a finite number of possible outputs. As expected, increasing the complexity of the simulation slowed down the learning. These simulations differed dramatically from the real data sets in two ways: (1) the number of categories ranged from 144 to 9216, whereas it was either 2 or 3 in the real data, and (2) the number of examples was 10,000, whereas it was from 100 to 300 for the real data. Thus the simulations show the behavior of EACH for larger scale, more complicated data sets.

The output (dependent) variable in the simulations was dependent on four to seven variables, although the simulation can be set to use any number of variables. In each simulation, one of the variables was independent of all the others, the remaining variables were interdependent. The simulation equations that actually determined the next price of a stock (the output variable) used two basic mathematical relationships: linear combinations of variables and threshold values. For most of the results below, the output variable y was related to each input feature x_i by a constant function with discontinuities; i.e., a step function. For example, the equation relating y to x_1 was

$$f(x_1) = \begin{cases} 25 & x_1 < 40 \\ 70 & 40 \le x_1 < 90 \\ 45 & 90 \le x_1 < 120 \\ 115 & \text{otherwise} \end{cases}$$

where $y = f(x_1) + f(x_2) + ... + f(x_k)$. In some of the simulation runs, linear rather than step functions were used for the $f(x_i)$. For those simulations where all the x_i were constant functions, the number of possible values C of the output variable is given by

$$C = \prod_{i=1}^{k} m_i$$

where m_i is the number of discontinuous regions of the step function

$f(x_i)$. This number C is the number of categories that EACH must learn for a given test run.

In the experiments below, I recorded data on success rates after every 50 examples. On each run of 10,000 examples, I took 200 data points, each of which measured the number of successful predictions on the last 50 examples. Thus, in each of the charts below, the vertical axis represents the number correct out of 50, or one-half the percent correct. The values of all features for the examples were real numbers, and no two examples were ever identical (although, of course, many examples belonged to the same category as other examples). For each set of data reported, I also include the value of the feature adjustment rate Δ_f. In general, rates that were excessively high caused the system to oscillate, and thus led to worse performance than lower, more gradual rates. In some instances, Δ_f had no effect at all – a value of zero gave results equally as good as a rate of 0.02 or 0.05. This may have been because the underlying simulation model itself weighted most of the features equally, so no feature weights were necessary.

4.4.1 Tests with four variables

This first run shown here used four input variables. The equations relating them to the output variable were constant functions with discontinuities; i.e., step functions. The number of categories C was 144. The expectation was that EACH would perform well despite the discontinuities – in fact, EACH should perform well *because* of them, when one compares it to other programs – and this expectation was borne out by the tests. (For this test and all the following ones, the system was seeded with 25 randomly generated exemplars. When other experiments were run using just two seed exemplars, EACH achieved nearly identical results.) The figures below display the performance rates, expressed as the number of correct predictions, for successive sets of 50 examples. For example, looking at the very first point of Figure 4.7, we see that for the first 50 examples, EACH had a 66% success rate (33 out of 50 correct). Later, on examples 451 through 500, it had increased to an

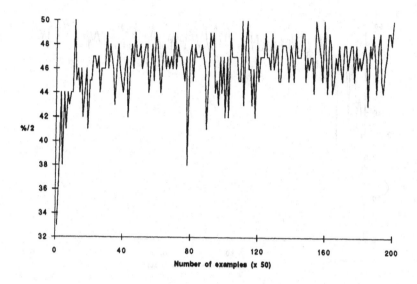

Figure 4.7: Four variables, $\Delta_f = 0$.

88% success rate. The learning curve fairly quickly approached 100%, although it occasionally missed a prediction even after several thousand examples. The oscillations in the success rate are probably due to the system initially growing some rectangles too large, causing errors that were only corrected after nested rectangles (exceptions) were formed inside the over-generalized rectangles. These oscillations get smaller as the system sees more and more examples. At the end of 10,000 examples, EACH had stored 215 exemplars during this test, including the seed set.

The feature adjustment rate seemed to have a small benefit for some of the trials. With $\Delta_f = 0.5$, the performance level was slightly better (though not significantly) than with $\Delta_f = 0$, and the system stored only 206 examples rather than 215. Figure 4.8 shows this result. The two curves are superimposed in Figure 4.9, showing the comparison

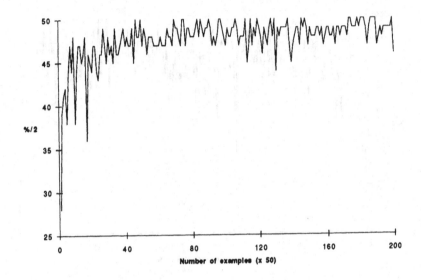

Figure 4.8: Four variables, $\Delta_f = 0.5$.

between the two tests.   The two learning curves in Figure 4.9 are almost the same, with a slight edge going to the results with $\Delta_f = 0.5$. The system was also run with Δ_f set to 0.02, 0.05, 0.1, and 0.75, and in all cases the learning curve was very similar, asymptoting towards 100% at about the same rate. The only difference was in the number of exemplars required, which reached a maximum of 417 with $\Delta_f = 0.05$. Even with 144 output categories, the system did not have much trouble learning this simulation. The following simulations, described below, were more difficult.

4.4.2   Tests with five variables

In the next simulation, the number of variables was increased from four to five, and the number of possible outputs C increased to 576. As expected, the learning rate decreased compared to the trials with four

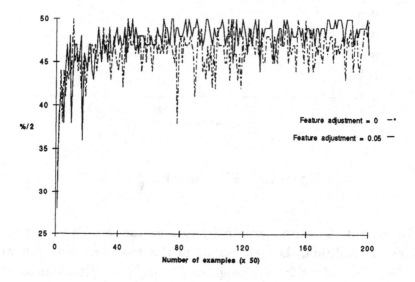

Figure 4.9: Performance comparison with four variables.

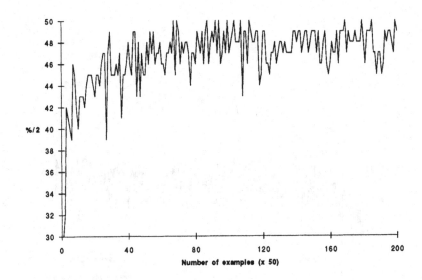

Figure 4.10: Five variables, $\Delta_f = 0$.

variables, but the system eventually reached the same level of performance. In addition, the best results in this trial were obtained with
no adjustment of the feature weights. The obvious explanation for this
finding is that the five variables all contributed equally to the value of
the dependent variable. Figure 4.10 shows the performance rates with
no feature adjustment, and Figure 4.11 shows a comparison between no
feature adjustment and setting $\Delta_f = 0.5$. In the comparison chart,
the two learning curves are nearly identical. For the simulation with
$\Delta_f = 0$, memory size was 273 after 10,000 examples. With $\Delta_f = 0.5$,
memory size was slightly larger at 345, making it the less preferable
model. Surprisingly, the minimum memory requirements for this trial
were only 30% greater than trial with four variables, despite the fact
that the number of categories increased by a factor of 5. One explanation for this result is that the examples were not uniformly distributed

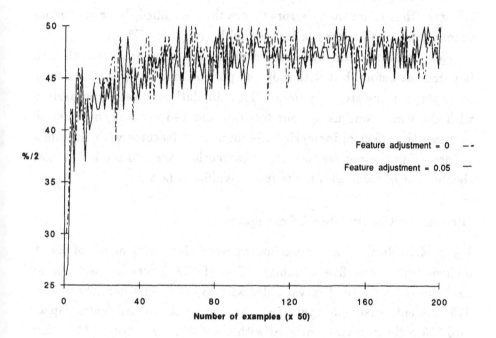

Figure 4.11: Performance comparison with five variables.

in feature space; rather, some areas had clusters of higher probability.

Notice here that the curves shown thus far display quite rapid initial learning, during the first 100 or 200 examples, and then more gradual improvement beyond that. This behavior is just what an exemplar-based learning model should produce: early exemplars fill large gaps in E^n, gaps that cause many errors before they are filled; later exemplars normally fill smaller gaps or less probable regions of E^n.

Next, a simulation was created using five input features, all step functions as before, but with only 144 possible outputs (i.e., there were fewer steps in the step functions). This simulation allows a comparison with the earlier one using four features and 144 outputs, in order to compare the effect of increasing the number of features with the effect of increasing the number of output categories. We will see below that the number of categories is the more significant factor.

Increasing the number of categories

Figure 4.12 displays a comparison between the performance of EACH on two tests using five variables. One of the curves is the same as that shown above for five variables with $\Delta_f = 0$, in which there were 576 different possible outputs, i.e., the simulation divided feature space into 576 regions, each associated with a different prediction. The other curve shows a test using five variables but only 144 output categories. We see from this figure that EACH performs better when there are fewer output categories. In the simpler simulation, the curve for the simpler simulation approaches 100% accuracy much more quickly, and it takes the other curve about 8000 examples to catch up.

Increasing the number of features

The comparison of categories versus features becomes more clear when we look at EACH's performance on two simulations of the same complexity with different numbers of features. Figure 4.13 shows the learning curves for two test runs, one in which there were five input features, and another with four features. Despite the difference in the number

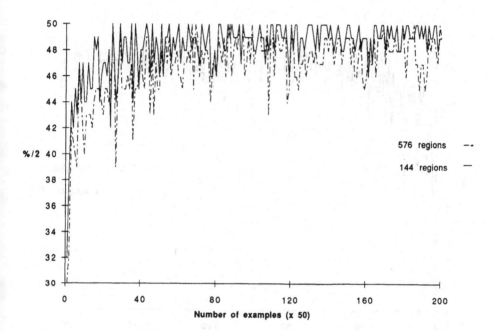

Figure 4.12: Different numbers of categories.

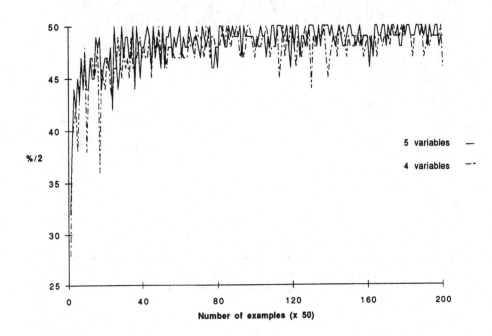

Figure 4.13: Five features vs. four features.

of features, the number of outputs was identical: both simulations had 144 possible outputs. The figure shows quite clearly that there is little or no difference in performance on these two tests. If anything, the system performed slightly better with five variables, at least during the first 1000 examples. Both systems asymptoted towards perfect performance. For this admittedly limited test, then, the number of output categories was more important in determining the performing of EACH than was the number of features.

4.4.3 Tests with seven variables

In the final set of tests using the simulation, two more input features were added to the model, bringing the total number of features to seven and the number of outputs to 9216. In other words, in these tests, the number of categories was almost equal to the number of examples. EACH was unable to reach 100% accuracy in 10,000 examples on this simulation. Figure 4.14 shows how well the system performed with feature adjustment set to zero and 0.02. The performance rate in these simulations dropped off somewhat, from 100% in the previous tests to just over 90% here. This is not surprising when one considers that there were 16 times as many categories. The size of memory required to achieve this performance level was also much larger: 844 exemplars with $\Delta_f = 0$, and 625 with $\Delta_f = 0.02$. Higher values of Δ_f did not improve performance. In this test, a small value of Δ_f produced the smallest memory model and a slightly better learning curve. In Figure 4.14, the performance with $\Delta_f = 0.02$ is clearly better for the first 2000 examples, and it remains better for the entire trial, although the two curves are much closer at the end.

Comparison with linear combination

Finally, I created a simulation model that used a linear combination of the seven input variables to determine the output variable. The formula was simply

$$y = k_1 x_1 + k_2 x_2 + \ldots + k_7 x_7$$

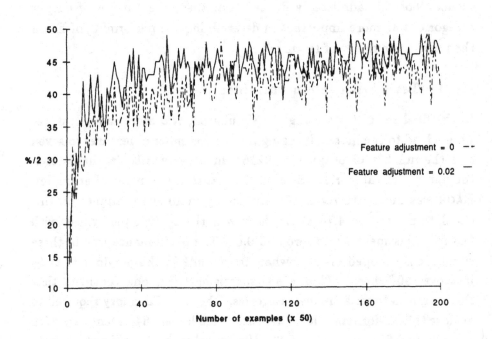

Figure 4.14: Performance with 7 variables.

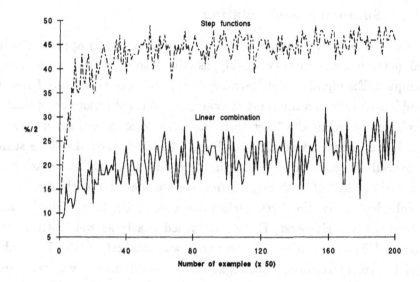

Figure 4.15: Linear combination vs. step functions.

where each k_i was different. Thus there were an *infinite* number of output categories. Since no prediction based on an exemplar could ever be exactly correct, EACH used the error tolerance parameter to determine if a prediction was correct. Recall that this parameter is expressed as percentage, and it indicates how much a prediction and an actual value may differ before the program considers the prediction incorrect. For this test, the allowable error was 3%. The results shown in Figure 4.15 used a setting of $\Delta_f = 0$.

Figure 4.15 shows the performance for this test compared to the performance with 7 variables using step functions. Not surprisingly, the program performed significantly better in the step function world. The obvious difficulty with a continuous output parameter is that an exemplar-based model must approximate every point on the curve with a different exemplar. The size of memory after 10,000 examples was

3748, much higher than on any other test. Clearly, a statistical regression model could perform better on a domain such as this one.

4.4.4 Summary of simulation

In most of the above tests, the system reached or closely approached its peak performance rate very quickly, usually within the first few hundred examples. Exemplar-based learning should produce this kind of result: rapid learning from a small set of examples. With the more complicated simulations used in the later tests, far more examples seem necessary in order to improve performance. Figure 4.16 shows, on the same scale, an overall comparison of EACH running with 4 variables, 5 variables, and 7 variables. The curves shown are the best for each simulation model. Naturally, the best performance was with four variables and 144 categories. However, EACH performed nearly as well with 5 variables and 576 categories. Performance was weakest on the 7 variable test. Interestingly enough, though, the 7 variable model was relatively parsimonious with memory – it used just 625 exemplars to capture all the 9216 categories. The reason this was possible was that the examples were not evenly distributed through feature space. Examples were much more likely to fall in some regions than in others, and many regions were so unlikely that they would probably not occur during a run of 10,000 examples. The feature adjustment rate was of some benefit in two of the three simulations (it did not help in the tests with five variables), although different values of Δ_f were optimal for different tests. This result indicates that further work needs to be done to determine the best method of adjusting feature weights. In all three simulation models, though, the performance of EACH asymptoted towards 100%. The curves shown here indicate that the NGE algorithm consistently converges towards a correct solution for the simulated problems.

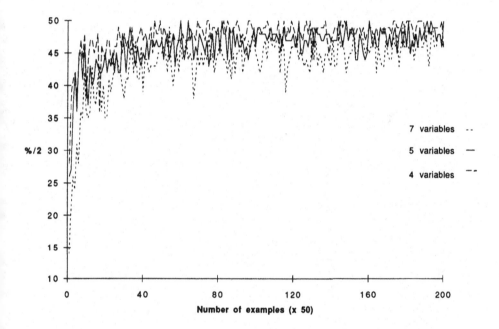

Figure 4.16: Performance with 4, 5, and 7 variables.

5

Conclusion

The experiments presented in this book demonstrate that an exemplar-based learning model that constructs hyperrectangles can learn effectively in a diverse set of domains. The EACH system displayed robustness in the face of both noise and incomplete data. Comparisons with experts' performance, where such comparisons were possible, were quite favorable, and in one domain – breast cancer prediction – the program performed significantly better than the experts.

Comparing the NGE learning model with learning theories that attempt to fit curves or hyperplanes to their data is difficult. In the echocardiogram results above, for example, the noisy, incomplete data set might be impossible to fit with a curve, and yet an exemplar model gives a perfect fit. For this kind of data, exemplar learning appears to do a much better job at *post hoc* data modeling than curve fitting models. On the other hand, an exemplar model, which is expressed as a set of data structures, is less concise than a curve, which can be expressed as a single function. In addition, it's unfair to compare a trivial exemplar model – one that contains all the examples seen – with a regression analysis; obviously, the trivial model will almost always fit the data perfectly. The NGE model contains generalizations (hyperrectangles), not just points, which makes such comparison a bit more reasonable.

A more appropriate comparison can be made between EACH and a concept learning model that creates descriptions in DNF form; e.g.,

$$(c_1 \lor c_2 \lor \ldots \lor c_n) \Rightarrow P$$

where each c_i is a conjunction of monomials, in which each feature is restricted to some fixed range of values (or, for binary features, simply restricted to true or false), and P is a prediction, either the name of a category or a real number. Each hyperrectangle in structured exemplar memory is equivalent to a single conjunctive expression of range inequalities. The breast cancer data allowed for exactly such a comparison, between EACH and AQ15. The comparison shows that EACH's performance is significantly better than the concept learning system. Both systems outperform human experts. The iris flower classification task allows comparison of EACH and a decision tree model, and here EACH came out roughly equivalent to the alternative model. These results confirm the usefulness and power of exemplar-based learning.

One of the strengths of the exemplar-based learning model is its extreme simplicity, in both the algorithm and the representation it creates. In its barest form, the exemplar model says to store every example as a single point, and to predict new points based on simple Euclidean distance to old points. As the experiments presented in this book illustrate, many modifications, such as weight factors and normalization of the axes, can be added to this basic notion, and the result is a fairly powerful, but still simple, learning theory.

The Nested Generalized Exemplar theory makes some very important modifications to the basic exemplar model. The most important issue in the NGE model is the construction of axis parallel rectangles – hyperrectangles – and the nesting of exceptions within these rectangles. The nesting of exceptions is relatively unique among machine learning models in AI – only Vere's [1980] system of counterfactuals resembles NGE, and that system dealt only with symbolic concepts.

The generalization process is also an important component of Nested Generalized Exemplar theory. The generalization rule that EACH uses is to increase the size of a hyperrectangle H whenever it is used to make a correct prediction for a new example lying outside the boundaries of

H. In addition, EACH was successful in most of the trials using the "second chance" heuristic, which looked at hyperrectangles that were the second closest exemplars to a new point. Some instance-based learning experiments conducted by Aha and Kibler [1989] use a more general variant of this heuristic, in which they consider the n nearest neighbors of a point. This n nearest neighbor approach uses the majority of the n points (which are not generalized) to make the prediction, instead of using a single exemplar. I tried this approach for the echocardiogram data, but found that results were worse than with either version of the EACH algorithm.

Another important contribution of the NGE learning model, is the fact that the hyperrectangles can be easily interpreted, when presented in a form such as Figure 4.6, by domain experts. This perspicuity is essential for any learning system that might be used by humans as a decision making tool.

5.1 Weight factors

An important issue, for both the theory and the implementation of exemplar-based learning, is the use of weights in the distance metric. Two kinds of weights were used here. First were the weights w_i on each of the feature dimensions, which were adjusted based on the successes and failures of the program's predictions. The results in the experiments presented here, especially the breast cancer prediction task, show that these weight parameters can significantly improve predictive accuracy. These results also indicate that the best performance is achieved by adjusting these weights slowly, using small values of Δ_f, since rapid adjustment causes the system to cancel the effects of earlier learning.

The experiments also indicate that different values of Δ_f might be better for different problems. One issue for near-term future research is how best to adjust feature weights. One hypothesis to test is that optimal performance might be achieved by allowing Δ_f to be gradually reduced over time until it reaches zero, in a manner analogous to simulated annealing in certain connectionist models. Additional experiments, with larger numbers of examples and longer runs, need to be performed to confirm this hypothesis. A new version of EACH currently under construction will run its own experiments to optimize Δ_f, and will be capable of using different Δ_f values for different domains.

The second kind of weights were weights on the exemplars (the hyperrectangles) themselves. This weight factor was added to the algorithm as a result of difficulties with the simulation experiments, and it resulted in considerable improvement. Very recently, Aha and Kibler [1989] have produced a noise-tolerant version of their instance-based algorithm which uses a factor very similar to EACH's weight factor in order to tolerate noise. Their algorithm keeps track, for each exemplar, of the percentage of the time an exemplar E is used to make a correct prediction. This is the same statistic tracked by EACH. If the percentages falls below a certain threshold, they assume it represents noise and erase it from memory. Aha and Kibler have also had positive results with their weight factor. Unlike their model, EACH never erases an exemplar, but the weight factor makes poor exemplars (i.e., one that make bad predictions) less and less likely to be used by the program.

One concern about all incremental learning algorithms is their sensitivity to the order of the inputs. The results I presented for the breast cancer prognosis problem demonstrated the variability of EACH when a data set was run through the system in different, randomized orders. Although the variability appears significant, it should become less so as the number of examples in the data set increases, and this is another area for future research. I hope that other researchers will also publish variability numbers, which will allow comparisons. One set of tests [Kinney 1988] using a commercially available version of a genetic learning algorithm showed slightly greater variability than EACH.

Additional experiments, using both real and simulated data, are being conducted to explore these issues and others in exemplar-based learning. Open questions for exemplar-based learning include how many variables the theory can handle before it begins to break down, either using too much memory or taking too much time to reach an acceptable level of performance. It has worked in the current set of experiments for up to nine features, or seven real-valued variables (in the simulated domain), but how will it perform when these numbers are doubled or tripled? What prevents the algorithm from reaching a 100% success rate on all domains? Is there some addition that would allow perfect performance? What if noise is absent from the data? Questions also remain about the nature of the domains that are well suited to exemplar learning versus those that are not. Classification problems, at least, are very well suited to exemplar-based learning. Future work will focus on both classification and other types of problems, from a variety of domains, in order to see how far this theory can be extended.

5.2 Synthesis with explanation-based learning

In Chapter 3, I discussed exemplar-based learning as a context free learning model, and contrasted it with explanation-based learning, which I called context dependent. The difference was in how much domain knowledge the respective theories use as they learn. Explanation-based learning often requires a considerable amount of domain specific knowledge in order to function at all in a domain. The domain knowledge is used to create an explanation, usually after a prediction failure, and this explanation serves as the basis for revising the program's rule base. Because of the amount of domain knowledge required, explanation-based learning systems usually process only a small number of examples: the knowledge required for each example must be entered by hand. NGE learning and other exemplar-based learning theories require little or no domain knowledge beyond a set of features and a dependent variable.

The value in combining the two types of models is that we now have the possibility of creating a learning system which starts with little knowledge, as the NGE model does, and can process and learn from any number of examples. In the future, we may be able to use explanation-based learning techniques to explain difficult examples, and possibly to discover additional features that should be added to the predictive model.

The idea behind combining the techniques is that a program would process the first few examples without attempting any explanations. As its memory grew, and it made fewer mistakes, the need for explanations of the failures would become greater. An explanation-based learning program might use the existing exemplar memory as the basis for explaining new examples that were not correctly categorized by the model. Such a combination presents an interesting developmental theory of computer learning.

5.3   Psychological plausibility

Given that the exemplar theory behind EACH originates in the psychological work of Medin and Schaffer, do the extensions to the exemplar model make sense psychologically? It is not the purpose or intent of this book to provide psychological results, but the hyperrectangle model does resolve some problems with the pure exemplar model. In particular, the hyperrectangle model compromises the pure exemplar theory with prototype theories, combining them into a multiple prototype theory. Each hyperrectangle represents a single prototype, but EACH is allowed to create many distinct hyperrectangles for the same category; i.e., multiple prototypes. As long as a hyperrectangle correctly predicts examples in its own neighborhood, it will continue to grow, which means that multiple prototypes can be of different sizes. Thus, when asked for a prototypical bird, a hyperrectangle-based system could choose the largest prototype and answer (for example) "robin." However, it would have no trouble recognizing a penguin as a bird, since that would match against a different hyperrectangle (the one for flightless birds). Furthermore, if I allow the system to remember a small number of specific examples (perhaps the most recent) inside each hyperrectangle, it could easily produce example birds on demand, as humans do.

5.4   Complexity results

Very recent results in computational complexity dovetail nicely with the hyperrectangle memory model constructed by EACH. In particular,

Helmbold, Sloan, and Warmuth [1988, 1989] have devised an algorithm which learns by constructing nested, axis-parallel hyperrectangles. The features used to describe each example must be real-valued, and the prediction must be binary. More significantly, their algorithm creates a *single* large rectangle containing positive instances, then a negative rectangle inside that, and a positive rectangle inside that, and so on. The problem domain is assumed to be one for which the true concept can be represented as a set of nested rectangles.

Given these constraints, which admittedly are quite restrictive, Helmbold *et al.* prove some very strong optimality results for their algorithm. In particular, they consider four optimality criteria: (1) the number of examples required to make accurate predictions with high confidence, (2) the probability of making a mistake on the nth instance, (3) the expected number of errors for the first m instances (using an incremental algorithm), and (4) the worst case number of errors for the first m instances. Their algorithm is optimal with respect to all these measures.

Note that the optimality measures do not say anything about the run time of the algorithm; Helmbold *et al.* assume a polynomial time algorithm is available. For empirical work such as this book (and other research) done in AI, the measures of Helmbold *et al.* are more important than run time measures. The most important feature of a learning algorithm, after all, is the accuracy of the concepts it learns.

The Helmbold *et al.* learning algorithm can apply to any intersection closed concept class. Rectangles are intersection closed since the intersection of any two rectangles is also a rectangle. Monomials and sub-spaces of E^n are also intersection closed. This constraint means that the "true" concepts in the class must be, e.g., rectangular. However, the representation constructed by the algorithm – a set of nested rectangles – is not constrained to be intersection closed.

The restrictions required for the proofs make this algorithm a very special case of the EACH algorithm. Helmbold, Sloan, and Warmuth are working on proofs of extensions of their algorithm that will remove some of these restrictions. For example, they are working on a proof of an algorithm that allows many distinct sets of nested hyperrectangles, instead of just one.

5.5 Future experimental work

Another extension of the exemplar learning model, and a natural next step for the EACH system, is to create a flexible, user-friendly system which allows a domain expert to use EACH to test ideas about interrelationships in a domain. For example, a medical researcher with a large database might wish to test various theories about the causes of disease, or the effects of certain treatments. He could use EACH to select a set of variables from the database, and then predict the variable of interest for a corpus of examples for which those variables fell within specified ranges of values. If the number of features were unmanageably large, the human's domain knowledge would serve to narrow down the set of possibly relevant features, and EACH could then be used to determine how good a model might be built with those features.

I am currently working to apply the EACH algorithm to several additional domains, all involving real data. In the process of modifying EACH to learn in these domains, I hope to create an interface which makes it possible for inexperienced users to operate the program and interpret its output. With a good interface, a machine learning program might become a test platform for ideas, in which the experimenter could select a small set of variables that the program would use to create an exemplar memory.

In the near future, I plan to run systematic experiments testing the performance of the NGE model in the presence of noise and irrelevant features. These experiments will use simulated data in order to control the experimental variables accurately. Noise can occur in either the input features or the feedback signals (the classification decision). For instance, noise can be introduced into an experiment by feeding the program erroneously classified examples. The program's performance can be measured as a function of the percentage of noisy examples. In addition, noise can be introduced by distorting the values of any or all features. Irrelevant features can be introduced in a similar manner, and performance can be measured as a function of the number of irrelevant features, or as a function of the percentage of irrelevant to relevant features.

As long as we lack proofs of the correctness or optimality of any machine learning algorithm, we will, and should, continue to explore many alternatives. The EACH algorithm represents an alternative that is simple to implement and undemanding of computer memory, and yet produces very good models. As with other learning programs, the best support for this one lies in its successful application to real data sets. The successful results described in this book provide an encouraging basis for further work and extensions to the NGE algorithm.

Appendix A

Data sets

This appendix contains the raw data used for the experiments reported in Chapter 4. The purpose of including the data is to allow others to use it to run comparative experiments. Each data set is listed as a simple list of examples, one example per line. At the beginning of the data set, I list the order of the variables and indicate which variable is the prediction.

A.1 Breast cancer data

The data for breast cancer patients included 14 variables per patient, several of which were not used. (They were not identified when I received the data, and were not used by Michalski in his experiments.) The prediction is the 12th variable in each line. The descriptions of the variables, exactly as they were give to me, are: 1 – age, 2 – menopause, 3 – not used, 4 – tumor size, 5 – inv nodes, 6 – not used, 7 – node caps, 8 – deg malig, 9 – breast, 10 – breast quad, 11 – irradiat, 12 – breast cancer, 13 – not used, 14 – not used.

```
39 1 39 30  0 12 2 3 1 2 2 2 0 0
41 1 41 20  0 19 2 2 2 3 2 2 0 0
40 1 40 20  0 11 2 2 1 2 2 2 0 0
65 2 43 15  0 12 2 2 2 1 2 2 0 0
```

```
43 1 43  0   0 10 2 2 2 4 2 2 0  0
65 2 58 17   0 11 2 2 1 2 2 2 0  0
53 1 53 25   0 13 2 2 1 2 2 2 0  0
60 2 45 20   0 11 2 1 1 2 2 2 0  0
53 1 53 15   0 13 2 2 1 2 2 1 18  1
46 1 46 50   0 16 2 2 1 2 2 2 0  0
41 1 41 20   0 16 2 2 2 1 2 2 0  0
48 1 48 00   0 11 2 3 1 5 2 2 0  0
51 2 49 25   0 20 2 2 1 2 2 2 0  0
67 2 37 10   0 13 2 1 1 3 2 2 0  0
47 1 47 40   0 11 2 1 1 2 2 1 28  2
57 2 55 35   0 11 2 2 1 2 2 1 34  3
51 2 41 25   0 17 2 3 1 3 2 2 0  0
47 1 47 30   0 21 2 3 1 1 2 2 0  0
62 2 32 30   0 13 2 1 1 2 2 2 0  0
47 1 47 15   0 15 2 2 1 2 2 2 0  0
52 1 52 30   0 11 2 3 1 2 2 2 0  0
62 2 50 30   0 14 2 3 1 2 2 2 0  0
59 2 57 30   0 13 2 1 2 3 2 2 0  0
52 2 51 40   0  9 2 2 1 2 2 2 0  0
62 2 50 15   0 11 2 2 1 2 2 2 0  0
39 1 39 25   0 13 2 2 2 2 2 2 0  0
50 1 50 40   0 10 2 2 1 1 2 2 0  0
54 1 54 35   0 14 2 2 1 2 2 0  0
46 1 46 25   0 12 2 2 1 1 2 2 0  0
50 1 50 20   0  8 2 1 1 2 2 2 0  0
62 2 47 25   0  9 2 3 2 1 2 2 0  0
41 1 41 40   0 12 2 2 2 2 2 2 0  0
65 2 48 30   0 13 2 2 1 2 2 2 0  0
51 1 51 25   0 11 2 2 1 3 2 1 35  5
31 1 31  0   0 20 2 2 2 5 2 1 39 14
52 2 49 40   0 12 2 3 2 1 2 2 0  0
59 2 53 30   0 15 2 3 1 0 2 1 9  6
51 1 51 15   0  7 2 2 2 2 2 2 0  0
```

```
55 1 55 10  0 20 2 3 1 2 2 2 0 0
57 2 47 10  0 10 2 1 2 1 2 2 0 0
54 2 47 10  0  7 2 1 1 1 2 2 0 0
36 1 36 30  0 10 2 2 1 1 2 2 0 0
56 2 49 00  0 15 2 2 1 5 2 2 0 0
55 2 53 15  0 22 2 1 2 5 2 2 0 0
44 1 44 10  0 18 2 2 1 2 2 2 0 0
41 1 41 30  0 14 2 1 1 2 2 2 0 0
54 2 53 23  0 11 2 1 2 2 2 2 0 0
67 2 51 25  0  8 2 2 1 2 2 2 0 0
68 2 53  8  0  8 2 1 1 5 2 2 0 0
41 1 41 10  0 14 2 2 1 1 2 2 0 0
59 2 48 50  0 11 2 1 2 3 2 2 0 0
59 2 48 30  0 11 2 1 1 1 2 2 0 0
45 1 45 25  0 12 2 2 2 2 2 2 0 0
52 1 52 25  0 12 2 2 1 3 2 1 27 7
52 1 52 25  0 11 2 1 2 1 2 2 0 0
49 1 49 20  0 24 2 1 2 3 2 2 0 0
52 1 52 30  0 15 2 3 1 3 2 1 37 1
42 1 42 20  0 10 2 1 2 2 2 2 0 0
47 1 47 35  0 19 2 1 2 1 2 1 36 1
55 2 39 15  0 11 2 2 1 2 2 2 0 0
34 1 34 20  0 14 2 2 1 4 2 2 0 0
51 1 51 15  0  7 2 1 1 2 2 2 0 0
70 2 50 20  0 12 2 3 1 1 2 2 0 0
70 2 45 40  0  1 2 1 2 1 2 2 0 0
55 2 48 00  0  0 2 1 2 5 2 2 0 0
50 2 41  8  0 13 2 2 2 3 2 2 0 0
63 2 50 30  0 15 2 1 1 1 2 2 0 0
65 2 50 15  0 15 2 1 2 1 2 2 0 0
47 1 47 20  0 12 2 2 1 5 2 2 0 0
43 1 43 10  0 13 2 1 2 4 2 2 0 0
54 2 52  0  0 12 2 1 1 2 2 2 0 0
29 1 29 35  0 12 2 2 2 3 2 2 0 0
```

```
40 1 40 25   0 14 2 1 1 4 2 2 0 0
43 1 43 12   0 11 2 1 2 1 2 2 0 0
41 1 41 25   0 15 2 1 2 4 2 2 0 0
52 2 50 20   0 15 2 3 1 1 2 2 0 0
45 1 45 22   0 14 2 2 1 2 2 1 9 8
51 2 49 35   0 14 2 3 1 2 2 2 0 0
60 2 54 50   0 13 2 2 1 2 2 2 0 0
58 2 51 20   0 13 2 2 2 5 2 1 30 6
47 1 47 30   0 19 2 3 2 3 2 1 11 1
61 2 58 10   0 11 2 1 1 2 2 2 0 0
51 1 51 25   0 26 2 1 2 1 2 1 20 2
47 1 47 25   0 13 2 2 2 1 2 2 0 0
62 2 50 20   0 17 2 2 1 1 2 2 0 0
50 1 50 16   0 15 2 2 2 4 2 2 0 0
36 1 36  8   0 15 2 2 1 4 2 2 0 0
54 2 52 12   0 10 2 1 1 2 2 2 0 0
57 2 54 10   0 14 2 2 1 2 2 2 0 0
34 1 34 25   0 17 2 1 1 5 2 2 0 0
50 1 50 25   0 15 2 2 1 2 2 2 0 0
46 1 46 25   0 19 2 2 2 5 2 2 0 0
54 2 47 12   0 17 2 2 2 2 2 2 0 0
66 2 53 10   0  6 2 1 1 1 2 2 0 0
62 2 43 18   0 14 2 2 2 2 2 2 0 0
58 2 46 15   0 12 2 2 2 2 2 2 0 0
45 1 45 20   0 16 2 1 1 4 2 2 0 0
53 2 50 35   0 12 2 3 1 1 2 2 0 0
65 2 50 40   0 16 2 2 2 2 2 1 28 2
46 2 45 20   0 17 2 2 2 1 2 1 37 8
63 2 50 25   0 15 2 2 2 2 2 2 0 0
57 2 50 20   0 11 2 2 1 1 2 1 21 7
73 2 50 00   0 11 2 1 1 4 2 2 0 0
52 2 46 20   0  7 2 3 2 1 2 2 0 0
40 1 40 40   0 15 2 1 2 1 2 2 0 0
32 1 32 00   0 11 2 2 2 5 2 2 0 0
```

```
53 2 51 20  0 15 2 3 1 1 2 2 0 0
51 2 50 25  0 13 2 2 2 1 2 2 0 0
63 2 52 22  0 14 2 2 2 1 2 2 0 0
54 1 54 10  0 18 2 1 1 2 2 2 0 0
45 1 45 30  0 17 2 2 2 4 2 2 0 0
60 2 42 30  0 19 2 2 1 1 2 2 0 0
63 2 45 15  0  9 2 2 2 1 2 2 0 0
47 1 47 30  0 13 2 1 1 3 2 2 0 0
36 1 36 25  0 15 2 2 1 2 2 2 0 0
49 2 45 20  0 12 2 3 1 2 2 2 0 0
57 2 54 30  0 18 2 3 2 2 2 2 0 0
53 1 53 25  0 15 2 2 2 4 2 2 0 0
44 1 44 15  0 10 2 2 1 1 2 1 12 4
44 1 44 20  0 14 2 2 1 4 2 2 0 0
47 1 47 10  0 16 2 2 2 2 2 2 0 0
64 2 54 30  0 14 2 3 2 5 2 1 35 1
46 1 46 30  0 14 2 1 2 1 2 2 0 0
49 1 49 20  0 10 2 2 1 1 2 2 0 0
37 1 37 40  0 11 2 2 2 3 2 2 0 0
48 1 48 30  0 12 2 3 2 3 2 2 0 0
64 2 49 30  0 13 2 1 2 1 2 2 0 0
57 2 40 27  0 17 2 1 1 2 2 2 0 0
54 2 53 15  0 20 2 1 2 5 2 2 0 0
47 1 47 20  0 14 2 2 1 2 2 2 0 0
47 1 47 10  0 11 2 1 2 1 2 2 0 0
45 1 45 35  0 10 2 2 2 3 2 2 0 0
54 2 43 23  0 19 2 2 2 1 2 2 0 0
38 1 38 15  0 10 2 1 1 2 2 2 0 0
47 2 41 20  0 11 2 3 1 1 2 2 0 0
36 1 36 10  0 19 2 1 2 2 2 2 0 0
68 2 55 15  0 15 2 1 1 4 2 2 0 0
61 2 51 20  0 19 2 1 1 2 2 2 0 0
54 2 42 15  0 17 2 2 2 3 2 2 0 0
58 2 47 40  0 10 2 3 1 1 2 2 0 0
```

```
31 1 31 15  0 15 2 1 2 2 2 1 17 2
54 2 49 30  0 17 2 1 2 2 2 2 0 0
41 1 41 25  0 13 2 3 1 3 2 1 58 8
66 2 49 10  0 16 2 1 2 2 2 2 0 0
74 2 49 10  0  5 2 2 1 5 2 2 0 0
39 1 39 30  7 11 1 2 2 3 2 2 0 0
36 1 36 30  1 10 2 1 2 1 2 1 24 1
36 1 36 25  7 26 1 2 2 1 1 2 0 0
54 1 54 25  2 11 1 2 1 1 2 2 0 0
46 1 46 35 10 14 1 2 2 1 1 2 0 0
45 1 45 40  5 13 1 3 2 1 1 2 0 0
46 1 46 30  8 17 2 2 1 1 2 2 0 0
60 2 50 28  2 10 2 3 1 4 1 1 15 1
54 2 53 40  1 13 2 3 1 3 2 2 0 0
63 2 45 30  1 13 2 2 1 2 1 2 0 0
66 2 56 22  1 13 2 3 2 2 2 1 9 10
32 1 32 25  3 21 1 3 1 2 1 1 24 6
49 2 48 20  3 12 2 3 2 2 1 1 9 1
49 1 49 30 15 15 1 3 1 2 2 1 3 6
39 1 39 20  3 16 2 2 2 5 2 2 0 0
51 1 51 30  1 15 2 3 2 1 1 1 9 6
35 1 35 40  3 16 2 3 2 3 1 2 0 0
68 2 53 40  5 16 1 3 2 2 2 1 4 6
60 2 44 45  1 11 2 1 2 3 1 1 15 1
51 1 51 50 11 16 1 2 2 1 2 1 36 10
45 1 45  8  2 14 2 1 1 2 1 2 0 0
47 1 47 30  5 17 2 2 2 1 2 1 15 10
35 1 35 30  3 11 2 3 2 1 1 1 9 12
38 1 38 40  1 15 2 2 1 2 1 2 0 0
70 2 45 15 11 11 0 1 1 2 1 1 12 8
48 1 48 30  1  8 2 2 1 4 2 2 0 0
59 2 56 40  3 14 1 2 1 2 2 2 0 0
51 1 51 20  3 13 1 2 1 2 2 2 0 0
63 2 51 10  1 10 2 1 1 1 2 2 0 0
```

```
48 1 48 45  1 13 2 2 1 2 1 2 0 0
62 2 56 45  7 13 1 3 1 5 2 2 0 0
40 1 40 25  1 10 0 2 1 4 1 2 0 0
69 2 53 30  1  8 2 3 2 1 1 1 20 8
54 1 54 25  3 10 1 3 1 2 1 1 48 8
43 1 43 25  2 13 2 2 2 2 1 6 1
67 2 50 50  2  9 2 2 2 1 1 2 0 0
32 1 32 35  2 12 2 3 1 2 2 1 6 6
51 1 51 30  3 10 1 2 1 2 1 2 0 0
33 1 33 20  2 10 2 3 1 5 2 2 0 0
49 1 49 20  4 13 1 2 2 3 1 1 35 8
66 2 53 20  3 18 2 2 1 2 1 1 37 2
50 2 39 30  2 12 2 3 2 1 2 2 0 0
55 2 53 25 17 22 1 3 2 1 2 2 0 0
63 2 50 30  5 16 1 3 1 2 2 2 0 0
54 2 50 35 16 19 2 3 1 2 2 2 0 0
61 2 48 18  1  5 2 3 2 1 1 2 0 0
44 1 44 15 17 19 1 3 1 2 2 1 6 2
56 2 52 25  8 10 2 3 1 2 1 1 20 3
33 2 22 15  2 20 2 3 2 1 2 2 0 0
62 2 50 40  3 14 2 2 2 1 1 2 0 0
58 2 49 24  4 19 1 3 2 3 2 1 59 8
52 2 48 25  5 12 1 3 2 1 2 2 0 0
52 1 52 30  1 11 2 1 1 5 2 2 0 0
56 2 52 30  2 15 2 1 2 5 2 2 0 0
45 1 45 35  2 16 2 1 1 2 2 2 0 0
49 1 49 30 13 16 1 3 1 1 1 1 51 6
46 1 46 27  2 15 2 3 2 1 1 2 0 0
35 1 35 30 10 16 2 2 2 1 1 1 25 7
46 1 46 30  3 19 1 2 2 2 2 2 0 0
61 2 52 10  1 17 2 2 2 1 1 2 0 0
63 2 50 28  5 12 0 1 2 1 1 2 0 0
48 1 48 20  5 12 2 2 2 1 2 2 0 0
49 2 45 40 16 18 1 2 2 1 1 2 0 0
```

```
51 1 51 12   1 14 2 2 2 1 2 2 0 0
38 1 38 18   8  9 1 3 1 2 1 1 1 10 3
47 2 45 30   1 17 2 2 1 1 1 2 0 0
35 1 35 20   3 22 1 2 2 1 1 2 0 0
37 1 37 15   1 14 2 1 1 2 2 2 0 0
57 2 52 30  11 18 1 3 1 4 1 1 12 8
65 2 41 30   7 12 1 2 2 3 2 2 0 0
60 2 53 35   6 16 1 3 1 2 2 1 24 2
52 2 46 20   3  8 1 2 2 1 2 2 0 0
31 1 31 20   5 14 1 2 1 2 2 1 27 14
43 1 43 28   1 13 2 3 1 1 2 1 9 1
43 1 43 50   2 13 2 2 2 2 1 1 56 9
36 1 36 40   1 10 2 1 1 1 2 1 21 2
63 2 52 50   1 13 2 3 2 1 2 1 12 2
50 1 50 25   3 21 1 2 1 2 1 2 0 0
48 1 48 30   1 18 2 2 2 3 1 2 0 0
42 1 42 30   2 14 1 3 2 3 2 1 23 2
40 1 40 30   6 21 1 3 2 1 2 1 24 7
44 1 44 32   1 12 2 1 1 2 1 1 43 6
43 1 43 20   4 19 1 2 1 2 1 1 8 3
48 2 42 25   1 11 2 2 1 2 2 2 0 0
57 1 54 30   8 10 1 2 1 4 1 1 41 9
53 2 50 30   4 22 2 3 2 1 2 1 12 14
68 2 51 12   2 15 2 2 1 2 2 2 0 0
65 2 51 25   4 10 2 2 2 3 2 1 15 7
55 1 55 25   5 13 2 2 2 1 1 2 0 0
44 1 44 20   2 12 2 3 2 2 1 2 0 0
49 2 46 25  14 14 1 3 1 4 1 1 27 8
64 2 50 25   1 11 2 3 1 1 2 1 45 9
45 1 45 35   2 10 1 3 2 1 1 2 0 0
43 1 43 25   1 10 2 1 2 2 1 2 0 0
57 2 47 30  10 10 0 3 1 1 1 2 0 0
53 2 30 20   1 13 0 1 1 1 2 1 27 8
43 1 43 20   8 11 2 2 2 2 1 2 0 0
```

```
55 2 51 25  1  6 2 1 1 4 2 2 0 0
36 1 36 35  9 13 1 3 1 2 2 1 8 2
65 2 45 15  1 16 2 2 1 1 1 2 0 0
46 1 46 10  2 17 2 2 2 1 2 2 0 0
55 2 50 20  1 13 1 2 2 1 2 2 0 0
46 1 46 30  3 22 1 2 1 3 2 1 16 8
65 2 55 20 25 25 1 3 1 2 1 1 5 2
30 1 30 35  2 19 2 3 1 2 2 1 10 18
43 1 43 25  2 10 2 2 1 2 1 1 15 7
52 2 50 30  7 18 1 3 1 4 2 1 5 7
41 1 41 15 13 14 2 3 2 4 1 2 0 0
53 1 53 25  1 15 2 3 2 2 1 1 21 14
47 1 47 15  2 13 1 3 2 1 2 1 43 9
40 1 40 25  1 10 2 2 1 1 1 2 0 0
62 2 52 30  2 14 1 2 2 3 1 1 21 8
59 2 50 30  7 15 1 2 1 2 2 2 0 0
66 2 53 30  3 14 1 2 1 5 1 1 57 6
33 1 33 11  1 17 2 2 1 4 2 2 0 0
51 1 51 50  2 17 1 2 2 1 1 2 0 0
52 2 50 35  1  0 2 2 1 1 2 2 0 0
46 1 46 25  9 16 1 3 2 1 2 1 15 2
37 1 37 25  6 14 1 3 1 4 1 1 42 4
63 2 48 13  6 13 1 3 1 1 1 1 27 8
54 1 54 35 15 23 1 3 2 3 2 1 10 7
52 2 47 40  6 10 1 3 1 2 1 1 16 6
52 2 47 40  6 10 1 3 1 2 1 1 16 1
50 1 50 10  4 11 2 1 2 1 2 2 0 0
41 1 41 10  1 11 2 2 1 2 1 2 0 0
50 2 48 15  1  3 1 2 1 5 1 2 0 0
35 1 35 30  2 10 2 2 1 1 2 1 39 9
55 1 55 25  0 15 2 1 1 2 2 2 0 0
37 1 37 20  2 14 2 3 1 1 1 1 34 7
65 2 54 25  2 11 2 3 2 2 2 2 0 0
63 2 48 20  1 10 2 1 2 1 2 1 35 1
```

```
45 2 44 30   3 13 2 3 1 2 2 1 26 8
56 2 51 30   5 24 2 3 1 2 2 1 4 6
```

A.2   Iris data

The iris data is the simplest data set. The first item in each line below is
the category prediction, one of setosa, virginica, or versicolor. The next
four variables are: sepal length, sepal width, petal length, and petal
width.

```
setosa 50 33 14 02
virginica 64 28 56 22
versicolor 65 28 46 15
virginica 67 31 56 24
virginica 63 28 51 15
setosa 46 34 14 03
virginica 69 31 51 23
versicolor 62 22 45 15
versicolor 59 32 48 18
setosa 46 36 10 02
versicolor 61 30 46 14
versicolor 60 27 51 16
virginica 65 30 52 20
versicolor 56 25 39 11
virginica 65 30 55 18
virginica 58 27 51 19
virginica 68 32 59 23
setosa 51 33 17 05
versicolor 57 28 45 13
virginica 62 34 54 23
virginica 77 38 67 22
versicolor 63 33 47 16
virginica 67 33 57 25
virginica 76 30 66 21
virginica 49 25 45 17
```

setosa 55 35 13 02
virginica 67 30 52 23
versicolor 70 32 47 14
versicolor 64 32 45 15
versicolor 61 28 40 13
setosa 48 31 16 02
virginica 59 30 51 18
versicolor 55 24 38 11
virginica 63 25 50 19
virginica 64 32 53 23
setosa 52 34 14 02
setosa 49 36 14 01
versicolor 54 30 45 15
virginica 79 38 64 20
setosa 44 32 13 02
virginica 67 33 57 21
setosa 50 35 16 06
versicolor 58 26 40 12
setosa 44 30 13 02
virginica 77 28 67 20
virginica 63 27 49 18
setosa 47 32 16 02
versicolor 55 26 44 12
versicolor 50 23 33 10
virginica 72 32 60 18
setosa 48 30 14 03
setosa 51 38 16 02
virginica 61 30 49 18
setosa 48 34 19 02
setosa 50 30 16 02
setosa 50 32 12 02
virginica 61 26 56 14
virginica 64 28 56 21
setosa 43 30 11 01

setosa 58 40 12 02
setosa 51 38 19 04
versicolor 67 31 44 14
virginica 62 28 48 18
setosa 49 30 14 02
setosa 51 35 14 02
versicolor 56 30 45 15
versicolor 58 27 41 10
setosa 50 34 16 04
setosa 46 32 14 02
versicolor 60 29 45 15
versicolor 57 26 35 10
setosa 57 44 15 04
setosa 50 36 14 02
virginica 77 30 61 23
virginica 63 34 56 24
virginica 58 27 51 19
versicolor 57 29 42 13
virginica 72 30 58 16
setosa 54 34 15 04
setosa 52 41 15 01
virginica 71 30 59 21
virginica 64 31 55 18
virginica 60 30 48 18
virginica 63 29 56 18
versicolor 49 24 33 10
versicolor 56 27 42 13
versicolor 57 30 42 12
setosa 55 42 14 02
setosa 49 31 15 02
virginica 77 26 69 23
virginica 60 22 50 15
setosa 54 39 17 04
versicolor 66 29 46 13

versicolor 52 27 39 14
versicolor 60 34 45 16
setosa 50 34 15 02
setosa 44 29 14 02
versicolor 50 20 35 10
versicolor 55 24 37 10
versicolor 58 27 39 12
setosa 47 32 13 02
setosa 46 31 15 02
virginica 69 32 57 23
versicolor 62 29 43 13
virginica 74 28 61 19
versicolor 59 30 42 15
setosa 51 34 15 02
setosa 50 35 13 03
virginica 56 28 49 20
versicolor 60 22 40 10
virginica 73 29 63 18
virginica 67 25 58 18
setosa 49 31 15 01
versicolor 67 31 47 15
versicolor 63 23 44 13
setosa 54 37 15 02
versicolor 56 30 41 13
versicolor 63 25 49 15
versicolor 61 28 47 12
versicolor 64 29 43 13
versicolor 51 25 30 11
versicolor 57 28 41 13
virginica 65 30 58 22
virginica 69 31 54 21
setosa 54 39 13 04
setosa 51 35 14 03
virginica 72 36 61 25

```
virginica 65 32 51 20
versicolor 61 29 47 14
versicolor 56 29 36 13
versicolor 69 31 49 15
virginica 64 27 53 19
virginica 68 30 55 21
versicolor 55 25 40 13
setosa 48 34 16 02
setosa 48 30 14 01
setosa 45 23 13 03
virginica 57 25 50 20
setosa 57 38 17 03
setosa 51 38 15 03
versicolor 55 23 40 13
versicolor 66 30 44 14
versicolor 68 28 48 14
setosa 54 34 17 02
setosa 51 37 15 04
setosa 52 35 15 02
virginica 58 28 51 24
versicolor 67 30 50 17
virginica 63 33 60 25
setosa 53 37 15 02
```

A.3   Echocardiogram data

The echocardiogram data is more complicated than the previous sets,
and needs considerable filtering before it can be used. Anyone wishing
to use this data should contact the author. There are 13 variables per
patient. Some of them, such as the patient name, are obviously not
useful for predicting recurrence of heart attacks, and were not used in
my experiments. For many patients, one or more variables are missing.
Such missing values are indicated by a * below.

The variables, in order, are: (1) how long the patient survived after the echocardiogram, (2) whether or not the patient was alive at the end of the survival period indicated by variable 1 (0 means alive, 1 means dead), (3) the age of the patient when the heart attack occurred, (4) whether or not the patient had pericardial effusion (0 means no), (5) fractional shortening, (6) minimal mitral E-point septal separation, (7) left ventricular end-diastolic dimension, (8) wall motion score, (9) wall motion index, (10) ignore, (11) name (replaced by "x" to preserve privacy), (12) group, and (13) whether or not the patient was alive after one year (1 means alive, 0 means either dead or followed less than one year).

```
11 0 71 0 0.260 9 4.6 14 1 1 x 1 0
19 0 72 0 0.380 6 4.1 14 1.70 0.588 x 1 0
16 0 55 0 0.260 4 3.420 14 1 1 x 1 0
57 0 60 0 0.253 12.062 4.603 16 1.450 0.788 x 1 0
19 1 57 0 0.160 22 5.750 18 2.250 0.571 x 1 0
26 0 68 0 0.260 5 4.310 12 1 0.857 x 1 0
13 0 62 0 0.230 31 5.430 22.50 1.875 0.857 x 1 0
50 0 60 0 0.330 8 5.250 14 1 1 x 1 0
19 0 46 0 0.340 0 5.090 16 1.140 1.003 x 1 0
25 0 54 0 0.140 13 4.490 15.50 1.190 0.930 x 1 0
10 1 77 0 0.130 16 4.230 18 1.80 0.714 x 1 1
52 0 62 1 0.450 9 3.60 16 1.140 1.003 x 1 0
52 0 73 0 0.330 6 4 14 1 1 x 1 0
44 0 60 0 0.150 10 3.730 14 1 1 x 1 0
0.50 1 62 0 0.120 23 5.80 11.670 2.330 0.358 x 1 1
24 0 55 1 0.250 12.063 4.290 14 1 1 x 1 0
0.50 1 69 1 0.260 11 4.650 18 1.640 0.784 x 1 1
0.50 1 62.529 1 0.070 20 5.20 24 2 0.857 x 1 1
22 1 66 0 0.090 17 5.819 8 1.333 0.429 x 1 0
1 1 66 1 0.220 15 5.40 27 2.250 0.857 x 1 1
0.750 1 69 0 0.150 12 5.390 19.50 1.625 0.857 x 1 1
0.750 1 85 1 0.180 19 5.460 13.830 1.380 0.710 x 1 1
0.50 1 73 0 0.230 12.733 6.060 7.50 1.50 0.360 x 1 1
5 1 71 0 0.170 0 4.650 8 1 0.570 x 1 1
```

48.0 0 64 0 0.190 5.90 3.480 10 1.110 0.640 x 2 *
29 0 54 0 0.30 7 3.850 10 1.667 0.430 x 2 *
29.0 0 35 0 0.30 5 4.170 14 1 1 x 2 *
29.0 0 55 0 * 7 * 2 1 2 x 2 *
0.25 1 75 0 * * * * 1 * x 2 *
36 0 55 1 0.210 4.20 4.160 14 1.560 0.640 x 2 0
1.0 1.0 65 0 0.150 * 5.050 10 1 0.710 x 2 *
1.0 1 52 1 0.170 17.20 5.320 14 1.170 0.857 x 2 *
0.03 1 * 0 * 12 * 6 3 0.140 x 2 *
27.0 0 47 0 0.40 5.120 3.10 12 1 0.857 x 2 *
35 0 63 0 * 10 * 14 1.170 0.857 x 2 0
26 0 61 0 0.610 13.10 4.070 13 1.625 0.571 x 2 0
16 0 63 1 * * 5.310 5 1 0.357 x 2 0
1 1 65 0 0.060 23.60 * 21.50 2.150 0.714 x 2 1
19 0 68 0 0.510 * 3.880 15 1.670 0.640 x 2 0
31.0 0 80 0 0.410 5.40 4.360 * 1 * x 2 *
32 0 54 0 0.350 9.30 3.630 11 1.222 0.640 x 2 0
16 0 70 1 0.270 4.70 4.490 22 2 0.786 x 2 0
40 0 79 0 0.150 17.50 4.270 13 1.30 0.714 x 2 0
46 0 56 0 0.330 * 3.590 14 1 1 x 2 0
2.0 1 67 1 0.440 9 3.960 17.50 1.450 0.857 x 2 *
37.0 0 64 0 0.090 * * 12 2 0.428 x 2 *
19.50 1 81 0 0.120 * * 9 1.250 0.570 x 2 0
20 1 59 0 0.030 21.30 6.290 17 1.310 0.928 x 2 0
0.250 1 63 1 * * * 23 2.30 0.714 x 2 1 * *
77 * * * * * 2 * x 2 *
2 1 56 1 0.040 14 5 * * * x 2 1
7 1 61 1 0.270 * * 9 1.50 0.428 x 2 1
10.0 0 57 0 0.240 14.80 5.260 18 1.380 0.812 x 2 *
12 0 58 0 0.30 9.40 3.490 14 1 1 x 2 0
1 1 60 0 0.010 24.60 5.650 39 3 0.928 x 2 1
10 0 66 0 0.290 15.60 6.150 14 1 1 x 2 0
45 0 63 0 0.15 13 4.57 13 1.08 .857 x 2 0
22 0 57 0 0.13 18.6 4.37 12.33 1.37 .642 x 2 0

53 0 70 0 0.10 9.8 5.30 23 2.30 .714 x 2 0
38 0 68 0 .29 * 4.41 14 1.167 0.857 x 2 *
26 0 79 0 .17 11.9 5.15 10.5 1.05 .714 x 2 0
9 0 73 0 .12 * 6.78 16.67 1.39 .857 x 2 *
26 0 72 0 .187 12 5.02 13 1.18 .785 x 2 0
0.5 1 59 0 .13 16.4 4.96 17.83 1.37 .928 x 2 *
12 0 67 1 .11 10.3 4.68 11 1 .785 x 2 *
49 0 51 0 .16 13.2 5.26 11 1.0 .786 x 2 0
0.75 1 50 0 .14 11.4 4.75 10 2.5 .28 x 2 *
49 0 70 1 .25 9.7 5.57 5.5 1.10 .357 x 2 0
47 0 65 0 .36 8.8 5.78 12 1 .857 x 2 0
41 0 78 0 .06 16.1 5.62 13.67 1.367 .714 x 2 0
.25 1 86 0 .225 12.2 5.20 24 2.18 .786 x 2 1
33 0 56 0 .25 11 4.72 11 1.0 .785 x 2 0
29 0 60 0 .12 10.2 4.31 15 1.67 .64 x 2 0
41 0 59 0 .29 7.5 4.75 13 1.08 .857 x 2 0
26 0 50 0 .06 30.1 5.95 21.5 2.39 .643 x 2 *
15 0 54 0 .217 17.9 4.54 16.5 1.18 1.0 x 2 0
.25 1 68 0 .22 21.7 4.85 15 1.15 .928 x 2 *
.03 1 * 0 .26 19.4 4.77 21 2.1 .714 x 2 1
12 0 64 0 .20 7.1 4.58 14 1.0 1.0 x 2 0
32 0 63 0 .20 5 5.20 8 1 .57 x 2 *
32 0 65 0 .06 23.6 6.74 12 1.09 .785 x 2 *
27 0 54 1 .07 16.8 4.16 18 1.5 .857 x 2 0
23 0 62 0 .25 6.0 4.48 11 1.0 .786 x 2 *
0.75 1 78 0 .05 10.0 4.44 15 1.36 .786 x 2 1
0.75 1 61 0 * * * 28 2.33 .857 x 2 1
34 0 52 0 .14 25 6.21 11.5 1.15 .714 x 2 *
1.0 1 73 0 .05 14.8 4.14 15.5 1.41 .786 x 2 *
21 1 70 1 .16 19.2 5.25 11 1.0 .786 x 2 *
55 0 55 0 .28 5.5 4.48 22 1.83 .857 x 2 0
15 1 60 0 .18 8.7 4.56 13.5 1.04 .928 x 2 *
0.5 1 67 0 .155 11.3 5.16 13 1.0 .928 x 2 *
35 0 64 0 .30 6.6 4.36 14 1.27 .786 x 2 *

53 0 59 0 .344 9.1 4.04 9 1.0 .643 x 2 0
33 0 46 0 .272 16.5 5.36 12.67 1.06 .857 x 2 *
* 1 61 0 .20 9.4 4.02 15.67 1.42 .786 x 2 1
33 0 63 0 .25 5.6 3.87 18 1.50 .857 x 2 *
40 1 74 0 .20 4.8 4.56 12.5 1.04 .857 x 2 0
33 0 59 0 .50 9.1 3.42 18 1.5 .857 x 2 *
5 1 65 1 .16 8.5 5.47 16 1.45 .786 x 2 1
4 1 58 0 .17 28.9 6.73 26.08 2.01 .928 x 2 1
31 0 53 0 .17 * 4.69 10 1.0 .71 x 2 *
33 0 66 0 .20 * 4.23 12 1.0 .857 x 2 0
22 0 70 0 .38 0 4.55 10 1.0 .714 x 2 0
25 0 62 0 .258 11.8 4.87 11 1.0 .786 x 2 *
1.25 1 63 0 .30 6.9 3.52 18.16 1.51 .857 x 2 1
24 0 59 0 .17 14.3 5.49 13.5 1.50 .643 x 2 0
25 0 57 0 .228 9.7 4.29 11 1.0 .786 x 2 0
24 0 57 0 .036 7.0 4.12 13.5 1.23 .786 x 2 *
.75 1 78 0 .23 40.0 6.23 14 1.4 .714 x 2 1
3 1 62 0 .26 7.6 4.42 14 1.0 1.0 x 2 1
27 0 62 0 .22 12.1 3.92 11 1.0 .785 x * *
13 0 66 0 .24 13.6 4.38 22 2.20 .714 x * *
36 0 61 0 .27 9.0 4.06 12 1.0 .857 x * *
25 0 59 1 .40 9.20 5.36 12 1.0 .857 x * *
27 0 57 0 .29 9.40 4.77 9 1.0 .64 x * *
34 0 62 1 .19 28.9 6.63 19.5 1.95 .714 x * *
37 0 * 0 .26 0.0 4.38 9 1.0 .64 x * *
34 0 54 0 .43 9.30 4.79 10 1.0 .714 x * *
28 1 62 1 .24 28.6 5.86 21.5 1.95 .786 x * *
28 0 * 0 .23 19.1 5.49 12 1.20 .71 x * *
17 0 64 0 .15 6.60 4.17 14 1.27 .786 x * *
38 0 57 1 .12 0.0 2.32 16.5 1.375 .857 x * *
31 0 61 0 .18 0.0 4.48 11 1.375 .57 x * *
12 0 61 1 .19 13.2 5.04 19 1.73 .786 x * *
36 0 48 0 .15 12.0 3.66 10 1 .714 x * *
17 0 * 0 .09 6.80 4.96 13 1.08 .857 x * *

```
21 0 61 0 .14 25.5 5.16 14 1.27 .786 x * *
7.5 1 64 0 .24 12.9 4.72 12 1.0 .857 x * *
41 0 64 0 .28 5.40 5.47 11 1.10 .714 x * *
36 0 69 0 .20 7.0 5.05 14.5 1.21 .857 x * *
22 0 57 0 .14 16.1 4.36 15 1.36 .786 x * *
20 0 62 0 .15 0.0 4.51 15.5 1.409 .786 x * *
```

Bibliography

Aha, D. and D. Kibler (1989)
Noise-Tolerant Instance-Based Learning Algorithms. *Proceedings of IJCAI-89*, 794-799. Detroit, MI, Morgan Kaufmann Publishers.

Bareiss, E., B. Porter, and C. Wier (1987)
Protos: An Exemplar-Based Learning Apprentice. *Proceedings of the Fourth International Workshop on Machine Learning*, 12-23. Irvine, CA: Morgan Kaufmann Publishers.

Barr, R. A., and L. J. Caplan (1987)
Category representations and their implications for category structure. *Memory and Cognition, 15:5*, 1987, 397-418.

Blumer, A., A. Ehrenfeucht, D. Haussler, and M. Warmuth (1987)
Learnability and the Vapnik-Chervonenkis Dimension. Technical Report UCSC-CRL-87-20, University of California, Santa Cruz.

Bourne, L. (1966)
Human Conceptual Behavior. Boston: Allyn & Bacon, Inc.

Bouthilet, L. (1948)
The Measurement of Intuitive Thinking. Unpublished doctoral dissertation, University of Chicago (cited in Posner, 1973).

Bradshaw, G. (1987)
Learning about speech sounds: The NEXUS Project. *Proceedings*

of the Fourth International Workshop on Machine Learning, 1-11. Irvine, CA: Morgan Kaufmann Publishers.

Breiman, L., J. Friedman, R. Olshen, and C. Stone (1984)
Classification and Regression Trees, Belmont: Wadsworth.

Bruner, J., J. Goodnow, and G. Austin (1956)
A Study of Thinking. New York: John Wiley & Sons.

Buchanan, B., and T. Mitchell (1978)
Model-directed learning of production rules. In Waterman, D. and Hayes-Roth, F. (eds.), *Pattern-Directed Inference Systems.* New York: Academic Press.

Bundy, A., B. Silver, and D. Plummer (1985)
An Analytical Comparison of Some Rule-Learning Programs. *Artificial Intelligence, 27,* 137-181.

Carter, C., and J. Catlett (1987)
Assessing Credit Card Applications Using Machine Learning. *IEEE Expert, 2:3,* 71-79.

Chase, W. and H. Simon (1973)
The Mind's Eye in Chess. In W. Chase (ed.), *Visual Information Processing,* New York: Academic Press.

Cover, T. and P. Hart (1967)
Nearest Neighbor Pattern Classification. *IEEE Transactions on Information Theory, 13:1,* 21-27.

Crawford, S. (1988)
Extensions to the CART Algorithm. *The International Journal of Man-Machine Studies.*

Danyluk, A. (1987)
The Use of Explanations for Similarity-based Learning. *Proceedings of IJCAI-87,* 274-276. Milan, Italy: Morgan Kaufmann Publishers.

DeGroot, A. (1965)

Thought and Choice in Chess. The Hague: Mouton.

DeGroot, A. (1966)

Perception and memory versus thought: Some old ideas and recent findings. In B. Kleinmuntz (Ed.), *Problem Solving: Research, Method, and Theory.* New York: John Wiley & Sons.

DeJong, G. (1981)

Generalizations Based on Explanations. *Proceedings of the Seventh IJCAI*, 67-69. Vancouver, B.C.: Morgan Kaufmann Publishers.

DeJong, G. (1986)

Explanation-Based Learning. Invited Talk, Fifth National Conference on Artificial Intelligence, Philadelphia, PA.

DeJong, G. and R. Mooney (1986)

Explanation-based learning: An alternative view. *Machine Learning, 1*, 145-176.

Dietterich, T. and R. Michalski (1983)

A Comparative Review of Selected Methods of Learning from Examples. In Michalski, R., Carbonell, J., and Mitchell, T. (eds.), *Machine Learning*, Tioga Publishing Co., 41-82.

Epstein, S. (1987)

On the Discovery of Mathematica Theorems. *Proceedings of the Tenth IJCAI*, Milan, Italy, 194-197.

Ernst, G. and Newell, A.

GPS: A Case Study in Generality and Problem Solving, Academic Press, New York, 1969.

Everitt, B. (1980)

Cluster Analysis. Gower Publishing Co. Ltd., Hampshire, England, 1980.

Fisher, D. and K. McKusick (1989)

An Empirical Comparison of ID3 and Back-propogation. *Proceedings of IJCAI-89*, 788-793. Detroit, MI: Morgan Kaufmann Publishers.

Fisher, R. A. (1936)

The Use of Multiple Measurements in Taxonomic Problems. *Annals of Eugenics 7:1.*

Franks, J. and J. Bransford (1971)

Abstraction of Visual Patterns. *Journal of Experimental Psychology, 90:1*, 65-74.

Heidbreder, E. (1946a)

The attainment of concepts: I, Terminology and methodology. *Journal of General Psychology, 35*, 173-189.

Heidbreder, E. (1946b)

The attainment of concepts: II, The problem. *Journal of General Psychology, 35*, 191-223.

Helmbold, D., R. Sloan, and M. Warmuth (1988)

Bootstrapping One-sided Learning. Unpublished manuscript.

Helmbold, D., R. Sloan, and M. Warmuth (1989)

Learning nested differences of intersection closed concept classes. In *Proceedings of the 1989 Workshop on Computational Learning Theory*, San Mateo, CA: Morgan Kaufmann.

Hinton, G. (1981)

Implementing semantic networks in parallel hardware. In Hinton, G. and Anderson, J.A. (eds.), *Parallel Models of Associative Memory*, Hillsdale, NJ: Erlbaum.

Hinton, G., J. McClelland, and D. Rumelhart (1986)

Distributed representations. In Rumelhart, McClelland, and the

PDP Research Group (eds.), *Parallel Distributed Processing: Explorations in the microstructure of cognition*, Cambridge, MA: Bradford Books.

Holland, J. (1986)
Escaping Brittleness: The Possibilities of General-Purpose Learning Algorithms Applied to Parallel Rule-Based Systems. In Michalski, R., Carbonell, J., and Mitchell, T. (eds.), *Machine Learning: volume II*, Morgan Kaufmann Publishers, 593-624.

Holland, J., K. Holyoak, R. Nisbett, and P. Thagard (1986)
Induction: Processes of Inference, Learning, and Discovery. Cambridge: MIT Press.

Iba, G. A. (1979)
Learning Disjunctive Concepts from Examples. AI Memo 548, MIT AI Lab.

Kahneman, D., P. Slovic, and A. Tversky (1982)
Judgement under uncertainty: Heuristics and biases. Cambridge: Cambridge University Press.

Kan, G., C. Visser, J. Koolen, and A. Dunning (1986)
Short and long term predictive value of wall motion score in acute myocardial infarction. *British Heart Journal, 56*, 422-427.

Kibler, D. and B. Porter (1983)
Perturbation: A Means for Guiding Generalization. *Proceedings of the Eighth IJCAI*, 415-418. Karlsruhe, West Germany: Morgan Kaufmann Publishers.

Kibler, D. and D. Aha (1987)
Learning Representative Exemplars of Concepts: An Initial Case Study. *Proceedings of the Fourth International Workshop on Machine Learning*, 24-30. Irvine, CA: Morgan Kaufman Publishers.

Kinney, E. (1988)
Personal communication.

Kolodner, J. (1980)
Retrieval and Organizational Strategies in Conceptual Memory: A Computer Model. Ph.D. thesis, Yale University (Research Report #187).

Laird, J., P. Rosenbloom, and A. Newell (1984)
Towards Chunking as a General Learning Mechanism. *Proceedings of AAAI-84*, Austin, TX: Morgan Kaufmann Publishers.

Laird, J., P. Rosenbloom, and A. Newell (1985)
Chunking in Soar: The Anatomy of a General Learning Mechanism. Tech Report #CMU-CS-85-154, Carnegie-Mellon University.

Larson, J. (1977)
INDUCE-1: An Interactive Inductive Inference Program in VL21 Logic System. Report UIUCDCS-R-77-876, Computer Science Dept., U. of Illinois.

Lenat, D. (1976)
AM: An Artificial Intelligence Approach to Discovery in Mathematics as Heuristic Search. Ph.D. thesis, Stanford University.

Lenat, D. (1982)
The Nature of Heuristics. *Artificial Intelligence, 19:3.*

Martin, C. and C. Riesbeck (1986)
Uniform Parsing and Inferencing for Learning. *Proceedings of AAAI-86*, 257-261. Philadelphia, PA: Morgan Kaufmann Publishers.

McQuitty, L. (1957)
Elementary linkage analysis for isolating orthogonal and oblique types and typal relevancies. *Educational Psychology Measurement, 17*, 207-229.

Medin, D. (1983)

Structural Principles in Categorization. In Tighe and Shepp (eds.), *Perception, Cognition, and Development*, 203-230.

Medin, D. and M. Schaffer (1978)

Context theory of classification learning. *Psychological Review, 85:3*, 207-238.

Michalski, R., J. Carbonell, and T. Mitchell (eds.) (1983)

Machine Learning, Tioga Publishing Co.

Michalski, R., I. Mozetic, J. Hong, and N. Lavrac (1986)

The Multi-Purpose Incremental Learning System AQ15 and Its Testing Application to Three Medical Domains, 1041-1045. *Proceedings of AAAI-86*, Philadelphia, PA: Morgan Kaufmann Publishers.

Mill, J. S. (1941)

A System of Logic. 8th edition (reprinted), London.

Minton, S. (1984)

Constraint-based Generalization: Learning Game-playing Plans from Single Examples. *Proceedings of AAAI-84*, 251-254. Austin, TX: Morgan Kaufmann Publishers.

Minton, S., and J. Carbonell (1987)

Strategies for Learning Search Control Rules: an Explanation-based Approach, 228-235. *Proceedings of IJCAI-87*, Milan, Italy: Morgan Kaufmann Publishers.

Mitchell, T. (1978)

Version Spaces: An approach to concept learning. Ph.D. thesis, Stanford University (CS-78-711).

Mitchell, T. (1983)

Learning and Problem Solving. Computers and Thought Lecture, *Proceedings of the Eighth IJCAI*, 1139-1151. Karlsruhe, West Germany: Morgan Kaufmann Publishers.

Mitchell, T., S. Mahadevan, and L. Steinberg (1985)
LEAP: A Learning Apprentice for VLSI Design. *Proceedings of IJCAI-85*, 573-580. Los Angeles, CA: Morgan Kaufmann Publishers.

Mooney, R., and G. DeJong (1985)
Learning Schemata for Natural Language Processing. *Proceedings of IJCAI-85*, 681-687. Los Angeles, CA: Morgan Kaufmann Publishers.

Needham, R. (1967)
Automatic classification in linguistics. *The Statistician, 17*, 45-54.

Osherson, D. and E. Smith (1981)
On the adequacy of prototype theory as a theory of concepts. *Cognition, 9*, 35-58.

Porter, B., R. Bareiss, and R. Holte (1989)
Knowledge Acquisition and Heuristic Classification in Weak-Theory Domains. Technical Report AI89-96, Artificial Intelligence Laboratory, University of Texas at Austin.

Posner, M. (1973)
Cognition: An Introduction. Glenview, IL: Scott, Foresman, and Company.

Posner, M. and S. Keele (1968)
On the Genesis of Abstract Ideas. *Journal of Experimental Psychology, 77:3*, 353-363.

Pritchard, N. and A. Anderson (1971)
Observations on the use of cluster analysis in botany with an ecological example. *Journal of Ecology, 59*, 727-747.

Quinlan, J. R. (1986)
Induction of Decision Trees. *Machine Learning 1:1*, 81-106.

Reddy, R. (1988)

Foundations and Grand Challenges of Artificial Intelligence. *AI Magazine, 9:4* (Winter 1988), 9-21.

Reed, S. (1972)

Pattern Recognition and Categorization. *Cognitive Psychology, 3,* 382-407.

Rose, D. and P. Langley (1988)

A Hill-Climbing Approach to Machine Discovery. *Proceedings of the Fifth Annual Conference on Machine Learning,* San Mateo: Morgan Kaufmann, 367-373.

Rosenblatt, F. (1958)

The Perceptron: A Probabilistic Model for Information Storage and Organization in the Brain. *Psychological Review, 65,* 386-407.

Rosenbloom, P. and J. Laird (1986)

Mapping Explanation-Based Generalization onto Soar. *Proceedings of AAAI-86,* 561-567. Philadelphia, PA: Morgan Kaufmann Publishers.

Rumelhart, D., J. McClelland, and the PDP Research Group (1986)

Parallel Distributed Processing: explorations in the microstructure of cognition, vol I. Cambridge: MIT Press.

Salzberg, S. (1983)

Generating Hypotheses to Explain Prediction Failures. *Proceedings of AAAI-83,* 352-355. Washington, D.C.: Morgan Kaufmann Publishers.

Salzberg, S. (1985)

Heuristics for Inductive Learning. *Proceedings of IJCAI-85,* 603-610. Los Angeles, CA: Morgan Kaufmann Publishers.

Salzberg, S. (1986)

Pinpointing Good Hypotheses with Heuristics. In *Artificial Intelligence and Statistics*, W. Gale (ed.), Addison-Wesley, 133-159.

Salzberg, S. (1988)

Exemplar-based Learning: Theory and Implementation. Technical Report TR-10-88, Aiken Computation Laboratory, Department of Computer Science, Harvard University.

Salzberg, S. (1990)

A Nearest Hyperrectangle Learning Method. *Machine Learning*, to appear.

Samuel, A. L. (1959)

Some Studies in Machine Learning Using the Game of Checkers. *IBM Journal of Research and Development, 3*, 210-229.

Shepard, R., C. Hovland, and H. Jenkins (1961)

Learning and memorization of classifications. *Psychological Monographs, 75*, No. 13 (Whole No. 517).

Sims, M. (1987)

Empirical and Analytic Discovery in IL. *Proceedings of the Sixth International Workshop on Machine Learning*, 274-280. Irvine, CA: Morgan Kaufmann Publishers.

Smith, E., and D. Medin (1981)

Categories and Concepts, Cambridge, MA: Harvard University Press.

Smith, E. and D. Osherson (1984)

Conceptual Combination with Prototype Concepts. *Cognitive Science, 8*, 337-361.

Sokal, R., and C. Michener (1958)

A statistical method for evaluating systematic relationships. *University of Kansas Science Bulletin, 38*, 1409-1438.

Thornton, C. (1987)

Hypercuboid Formation Behaviour of Two Learning Algorithms. *Proceedings of IJCAI-87*, Milan, Italy, 301-303.

Tou, J. and R. Gonzalez (1974)

Pattern Recognition Principles. Reading, MA: Addison Wesley.

Valiant, L. (1984)

A Theory of the Learnable. *Communications of the ACM, 27:11*, 1134-1142.

Valiant, L. (1985)

Learning Disjunctions of Conjunctions. *Proceedings of IJCAI-85*, 560-566. Los Angeles, CA: Morgan Kaufmann Publishers.

VanLehn, K. (1987)

Learning One Subprocedure per Lesson. *Artificial Intelligence, 31:1*, 1-40.

Vere, S. (1975)

Induction of Concepts in the Predicate Calculus. *Proceedings of IJCAI-75*, Tbilisi, Georgia, USSR: Morgan Kaufmann Publishers.

Vere, S. (1980)

Multilevel Counterfactuals for Generalizations of Relational Concepts and Productions. *Artificial Intelligence, 14*, 138-164.

Winston, P. (1975)

Learning Structural Descriptions from Examples. In P. Winston (Ed.), *The Psychology of Computer Vision*, New York: McGraw-Hill.

Wishart, D. (1969)

An algorithm for hierarchical classifications. *Biometrics, 25*, 165-170.

Index